FLOWERING BULBS

A CONCISE GUIDE IN COLOUR

FLOWERING BULBS

by
Ing. Eva Petrová

Illustrated by
František Severa

TREASURE PRESS

Translated by Olga Kuthanová

First Published in Great Britain in 1975 by
The Hamlyn Publishing Group Ltd.

This edition published 1989 by
Treasure Press
Michelin House
81 Fulham Road
London SW3 6RB

ISBN 1 85051 470 4

Printed in Czechoslovakia by PZ Bratislava

3/02/22/51-03

Contents

Foreword

Of the flowers that bloom in our gardens throughout the year the ones that are particularly outstanding for their clear, bright colours are those perennials that multiply by means of their underground parts — bulbs, corms, tubers or rhizomes — being collectively known as bulbous plants. They flower from early spring till late autumn. The dainty snowdrop has even become the very symbol of spring, and whether we come across it in a flower shop on a city street, in a garden or in a country meadow we have seen the first of the spring bulbs. Often by the end of February we can also admire the delicate crocuses and snow-flakes, later the squill, Glory of the Snow, muscari, brightly coloured tulips, hyacinths and daffodils. Their striking flowers make them a must in both the small and large garden, as well as in parks and public areas and they are also very popular for decoration in the home. Many are suitable for forcing and some are the best of all flowers for this purpose. Certain species are widely cultivated for this very reason and it is thanks to this characteristic that flowering bulbs are available practically the whole year round.

However, to have flowering bulbs in our gardens from spring till winter, it is necessary to grow a wide assortment. The most popular are the early-flowering species, which, however, soon fade and then dry up as the bulbs ripen. They are not very attractive during this period but this does not detract from their popularity for the garden would be quite drab and forlorn without them in early spring. The look of the garden need not suffer, however, if the fading plants are concealed by the leaves and flowers of later-flowering species. Thus, all depends on the suitable position of the various plants and on the proper selection of bulbous plants as well as other perennials.

Bulbous plants embrace a wide range including both small flowers suitable for the rock garden as well as tall ones that should be planted only in large gardens. Most have no special requirements and in central Europe can be grown practically everywhere. The only exception are certain type species, especially those native to the mountains, which require greater care and attention. These, however, are of interest only to the specialist.

Many bulbs are cultivated in a large variety of species and have been popular for centuries. Theirs is a long and rich history. Consider, for instance, the 'tulipomania', a craze such as happened with no other flower, which swept Holland in the sixteen-thirties. Overseas trade had brought great prosperity to the country and the wealthy burghers devoted much care to their gardens. Everyone wanted to have tulips in their gardens for these were the greatest vogue of the day. Interest in tulips grew at such a pace that soon they were being sold for exorbitant prices and became the target of speculators. Some bulbs cost as much as a merchant ship and according to one tale two houses in Amsterdam were sold to pay for three tulip bulbs. The spiralling boom in the tulip trade was followed by an even more rapid decline. In the year 1637 there were suddenly plenty of tulip bulbs on the market but no interested buyers. The craze had passed and tulips lost their popularity for a time. True tulip lovers, however, remained faithful to these flowers which soon regained the rightful place they hold to this day.

Some bulbs have their permanent adherents, organized in many countries in special clubs and societies, especially lily and gladiolus societies. Enthusiasts and collectors are not even deterred by the unsuccessful results of their efforts in their desire to have in their collections highly prized species, even though they be tender and difficult to grow. No amount of effort or money is too much for them to acquire newly introduced plants or rare type species which require the utmost care. For them, gardening thus becomes an expensive hobby and makes great demands on their time. For this reason beginners and in-experienced gardeners should select tried and tested varieties, ones that are hardier and require less care, if they wish to make gardening a relaxing pastime and pleasant change after a hard day's work. With little effort and even without adequate professional care such varieties will grow well, bear flowers and bring the gardener great joy and pleasure. This has been the guideline for the selection of bulbs presented in this book.

About Bulbs in General

Essentially, bulbous plants have but one feature in common: they all form underground storage organs. This grouping has no substantiation in the strict botanical sense; it is an arbitrary one created by practical growers inasmuch as all can be propagated by like means. This is also why there exist specialized horticultural establishments which grow only bulbous plants. In these establishments, growers can fully utilize such costly equipment as temperature-controlled store rooms, which are a must in the present-day cultivation of bulbs. In summer they are used to store hyacinths, daffodils and tulips; in winter, gladioli and the like.

From the botanical aspect it may be said that most bulbous plants are monocotyledons, a group where food reserves are stored in the underground parts far more frequently than in the dicotyledons. Most bulbous plants belong to the family *Liliaceae*, the formation of bulbs being a comparatively common feature of its various members which include *Allium*, *Erythronium*, *Fritillaria*, *Hyacinthus*, *Lilium*, *Scilla* and *Tulipa*. Other important families are *Amaryllidaceae*, which includes *Leucojum*, *Galanthus* and *Narcissus*; and *Iridaceae*, which includes *Crocus*, *Gladiolus*, *Iris* and *Ixia*. Dicotyledons are represented here only by the family *Ranunculaceae*, which includes *Anemone* and *Eranthis*; and the family *Primulaceae*, genus *Cyclamen*. Monocotyledons have other features in common. They do not have long main roots but a greatly branched network of lateral roots. The leaves are generally entire, narrow and with parallel venation. The flowers may be single, but are generally grouped into compound inflorescences. The individual flowers are simple and their parts are in multiples of three, that is they usually have six perianth segments, six stamens and three carpels. Sometimes, however, certain parts of the flower are transformed, for example the stamens or the perianth segments are doubled. This is how double forms are created. An important characteristic of bulbous plants is the comparative ease of vegetative propagation, generally by offsets from the bulb or tuber. Only a few are propagated more frequently by means of seeds.

Native Habitat

The bulbous plants presented in this book are mostly plants of the temperate zone for they are intended for growing out of doors in our gardens. However, only a few species can claim to be widespread throughout the whole of the temperate zone. As a matter of fact, many of them are endemics, that is they occur only in a given, specific location which is comparatively small. Of all the genera the most widespread are *Anemone*, *Fritillaria* and *Lilium*, the various species being found in Europe, Asia and North America. Primarily indigenous to Asia are *Eremurus* and *Puschkinia*. Southern Europe, the Mediterranean, Asia Minor and the area extending to central Asia are the home of the genera *Allium*, *Chionodoxa*, *Crocus*, *Eranthis* and *Tulipa*, as well as of *Colchicum*, *Cyclamen*, *Galanthus*, *Leucojum* and *Ornithogalum*, though the members of the latter group are also native to central Europe. *Narcissus* is native to the Mediterranean region but *N. pseudo-narcissus*, for instance, grows also in central Europe and the British Isles. Only in the warmer parts of the Mediterranean and in north Africa will we find *Arum*, *Hyacinthus*, *Muscari*, *Narcissus* and *Scilla* growing wild as well as *Gladiolus*, the most important species of which are native to southern Africa, and, in some cases, tropical Africa. Also native to South Africa are *Crocosmia*, *Eucomis*, *Ixia* and *Ornithogalum*. North America is the native habitat of *Camassia* and Central and South America that of *Tigridia*.

Most of these bulbs are hardy in European climatic conditions. This, however, is not true of gladioli and tigridias, which must be lifted in autumn and stored in dry, frost-proof premises for the winter, then planted anew in spring. Some species native to the Mediterranean countries, Asia Minor, Africa, China and Japan require protection against severe frosts. A protective cover is generally also required by alpine species even though they come from areas with harsh winters, for there they are covered by a thick blanket of snow in winter and the bulbs ripen fully during the hot summer season, thus increasing their hardiness.

Bulbs as Storage Organs

Bulbs and tubers, corms and rhizomes are all underground organs containing food reserves stored there by the plant during the growing period for the next growing season or for times of need.

In the wild, bulbous plants often grow in steppe, mountain, alpine or swamp areas where conditions for growth are optimum for only a short period as a rule, generally in spring, and they must therefore remain dormant for a long time. The reserve food materials stored during this brief vegetative period then provide for the rapid growth and development of the top parts of the plant. That is why bulbs can flower in spring as soon as the soil has thawed. The rudimentary flower is already fully developed in the bulb and all that is necessary for it to appear is adequate moisture in spring and a little warmth from the sun's rays. This property enables easy forcing of the plants. The growing period of most early-flowering species ends at the beginning of summer, by which time the plant has again prepared stores of food in the bulb and is ready to last out the dry, hot summer of the inland steppes and dry mountain slopes. During this time the bulbs continue to ripen and the various plant organs contained inside the bulbs continue to develop. With the arrival of cold autumn rains the bulbs start to make roots, but do not begin to grow, waiting instead for this under a cover of snow until the arrival of spring.

Bulbs, tubers, corms and rhizomes differ in their inner structure. A bulb is generally made up of a number of membranous layers — tunics — or else of fleshy scales whereas corms, rhizomes and tubers are solid in cross-section. Corms are the swollen base of a stem, usually rounded, and resemble a bulb in shape. Rhizomes are the swollen part of an underground stem, generally growing horizontally in the soil and often elongated and asymmetrical. Tubers are either swollen underground stems (stem tubers) or swollen roots (root tubers).

Bulbs, then, are generally tunicated. All the coats or layers grow from the base, called the basal plate. The outer coat or tunic varies in appearance, colour and thickness, depending on

11

the species of plant, and serves to protect the bulb from damage and drying out. Encased in the centre of the bulb is the young bud from which the flower will grow. Daughter bulbs form in the axils of the coats on the basal plate and the bud from which the new mother bulb develops is located under the inside coat. The roots grow out of the basal plate at the bottom. In the case of such bulbs the old bulb dies after flowering, a new mother bulb with lateral bulbs growing in its place. The daughter bulbs are held together by the roots until these have died away completely, after which they separate. Some species form daughter bulbs on stolons, which are underground stems, thus putting a greater distance between them and the parent bulb and providing them with more space and better conditions for successful growth. Tulips and camassias are examples of plants with tunicated bulbs as described above.

Hyacinth and daffodil bulbs also have fleshy tunics but do not die after flowering. Instead, they form new layers inside and only the outermost coat dies. Hyacinths bear offsets only if the bulb is very large and old or if the basal plate is damaged. Growers take advantage of this latter fact to promote the growth of daughter bulbs. Daffodils produce offsets every year but some do not part from the parent bulb and cannot even be detached. Often the outer tunic is firmly joined to the old bulb and does not part from it till the following year.

The bulbs of lilies are made up of separate scales arranged on a central axis. The outer tunic is absent and thus they are easily damaged, prone to drying out and do not stand up well to shipping and transplanting. The basal plate puts out persistent roots. New bulbs may be formed in various ways between the scales inside the old bulb, at the side of the bulb or on stolons of varying length depending on the species.

Bulbs are sometimes formed also in the axils of the leaves; occasionally this is true even of tulips, and then there are the aerial bulbs on the inflorescences of the genus *Allium*.

Most like the bulb in appearance are the rounded or flattened corms of gladioli and crocuses. Their surface is likewise protected against damage and drying out by an outer membranous coat. The colour, structure and thickness of the coat are often characteristic for the given species and help in its identification. These corms also die after flowering, a new one being formed each year on top of or beside the old one. A large corm will produce several small ones. Gladioli always form at least one new corm with small cormlets in a thick layer at its base.

Rhizomes and tubers form knobby eyes or buds from which new plants grow. Propagation in such cases is usually by division. For large-scale propagation they can be cut up into pieces, each with at least one eye. Rhizomes and tubers are persistent and are to be found in the genera *Trillium* and *Arum*, among others.

Cultivation

Most of the common bulbous plants are not difficult to grow, but the less experienced gardener will nevertheless do well to select only the well known species that have been tried and tested and are more or less certain to do well. A second must for success are good quality bulbs and tubers, ones that are healthy, undamaged and sufficiently strong. And thirdly, one must know the basic requirements of bulbous plants as well as the general rules of cultivation.

Bulbs grown in the garden are fairly adaptable and, except for the rarely cultivated species which are usually of interest only to specialists, the majority can be planted in a suitable spot in any garden.

Soil

The most suitable soils for bulbous plants are medium-heavy to light loam, clay or a mixture of clay and sand. Sandy or gravelly soil should never be chosen, for besides having an unsuitable structure, it also becomes too dry. Least desirable are heavy, cold and waterlogged soils where most bulbs suffer damage from fungus disease. In other words, then, the soil must be well drained and sufficiently deep, especially for species with large bulbs and tubers and for those that need to be planted at a greater depth. It should also be rich in humus and nutrients. The requirements of individual species show marked variation but in general it may be said that tall, robust plants with large leaves and flowers require more nutrients than small ones which can be grown on poorer soil, for example in the rock garden. If provided with insufficient nutrients the plants are not only weak and the new bulb or tuber slow to grow but in some cases, namely *Colchicum hybridum* and the like, they also produce fewer flowers. Very rich soil is a must for *Eremuras robustus*, and *Hyacinthus orientalis* and *Tulipa gesneriana* are also fairly demanding. Nutrients must be added to the soil in sufficient quantities, best of all in the form of well-rotted compost. Bulbs generally do not tolerate fresh compost or manure, but there is nothing against the use of artificial fertilizers.

Most species also need some lime and a soil that is neutral or slightly alkaline. Others, on the contrary, are intolerant of lime and require an acid soil, for example lilies (*L. auratum, L. japonicum* and *L. superbum*), which do not tolerate lime at all. *Lilium dauricum, L. speciosum, L. tigrinum* and the Bellingham Hybrids likewise do better in non-calcareous soils. A certain amount of lime in the soil, however, is a must for *Lilium candidum, L. henryi, L. longiflorum* and *L. martagon* and is advisable for most species of *Allium* and *Cyclamen*, which grow in calcareous soils in the wild.

Location

Most bulbous plants do better in a sunny location, though early-flowering species can also be grown with success under the open shade of deciduous trees and shrubs. In spring, when the trees are still leafless, the bulbs are provided with ample sun and after they have faded the light shade of the trees does not matter so much. Full sun is required by most members of the genus *Allium*, also *Crocosmia crocosmiiflora, Eremurus robustus, Eucomis punctata*, garden varieties of gladiolus, *Iris hollandica* and *Tigridia pavonia*. Most lilies, on the other hand, require light shade, in other words a spot that is shaded at least during the midday hours. As it is primarily the lower part of the stem that needs shade, in a sunny situation the problem may be solved by providing ground cover. Full sun is well tolerated by *Lilium bulbiferum, L. davidii, L. longiflorum, L. pardalinum, L. pumilum, L. tigrinum* and the Mid Century Hybrids. Shaded locations are a must for *Arum*. Also, the following plants do better in semi-shade: *Crocus byzantinus, Cyclamen europaeum, Erythronium dens-canis, Galanthus nivalis, Leucojum vernum, Ornithogalum umbellatum* and *Trillium grandiflorum*.

Another important factor is moisture, lack of which in a given location may be offset by watering and thus presents no problem in the ordinary garden. Greater care, therefore, need be devoted only to species with special requirements and in gardens where conditions are unduly dry. In general it may be said that all bulbs require moisture in spring during the growing and flowering period and for about a week after the flowers have faded to provide for the growth of the bulbs. During the summer months when the bulbs ripen most bulbous plants require a dry period, then moisture again in autumn when they put out roots. Most propitious to their growth is cool weather during the damp seasons in spring and autumn and hot weather in summer to ripen the bulbs. In a cool summer the bulbs and tubers are prone to mould. Some bulbs, however, require a damper location and in the wild are usually found growing in damp meadows, mainly *Bulbocodium vernum*, *Colchicum autumnale*, *Leucojum vernum*, and especially *Arum italicum*. A moister situation is good also for *Eranthis hyemalis*, *Galanthus nivalis*, *Ornithogalum umbellatum* and *Trillium grandiflorum*. *Eucomis comosa*, on the other hand, prefers a dry location, even one that is so dry as to be impossible for most other bulbs. Sensitive to ground moisture in winter are *Scilla sibirica*, most members of the genera *Muscari* and *Iris*, *Crocosmia crocosmiiflora*, *Cyclamen europaeum*, *Eremurus robustus*, *Tulipa gesneriana* and other *Tulipa* species.

Sheltered sites are best for bulbs, especially for those that are fairly tall and whose flowers dry out or are often damaged in a windy location. These include certain species of *Allium*, *Eremurus robustus*, *Eucomis comosa*, ixia hybrids, tall species of *Lilium* and *Tigridia pavonia*. Just as undesirable are deep hollows where some species are not only damaged by frost but, with the lack of adequate air currents, are also more prone to fungus diseases.

Some species need to be planted in a warm and sheltered position and might well have to be provided with a protective covering during the winter. For example, such lilies as *Lilium auratum*, *L. longiflorum*, *L. philippinense*, *L. speciosum* and *L. sulphureum*. Other plants include *Crocosmia crocosmiiflora*, *Eremus robustus*, *Eucomis comosa* and ixia hybrids. Garden varieties of gladiolus and *Tigridia pavonia* are always lifted for the winter and stored in a cool, dry place well protected against frost.

Preparation of the Soil

All bulbs should be planted in soil that has been well prepared beforehand, soil that has been ploughed or dug through, mixed

16

with compost and, in the case of poorer soil, supplied also with artificial fertilizers containing all the basic nutrients. The fertilizer should be applied at least two weeks before planting. Depending on the condition of the soil and the specific requisites of the given bulbs it may be necessary to add lime, peat or leaf mould. Very heavy soils should have sand, fine clinker or peat added. For some bulbous plants, especially certain tender lilies, it is a good idea to remove the heavy soil to a depth of 20 in., provide good drainage in the form of coarse gravel and return the soil mixed with whatever additions are required by the given plant. For most genera the soil should be dug to at least 8 in. for the bulbs and tubers require a layer of loosened soil to take firm root. In the case of genera with large bulbs or tubers and those which need to be planted at a greater depth it is necessary to dig the soil accordingly. This should be done at least a week before planting so that the soil has time to settle. The surface must also be well prepared. When planting, the soil should be sufficiently moist and in dry weather should be watered before the bulbs are put in.

For genera that are planted in spring it is necessary to prepare the ground, by ploughing or digging, in the autumn — a rule that applies to all garden plants. Only the addition of artificial fertilizer and surface treatment are performed in spring.

Planting

Bulbs may be divided roughly into four groups according to the period and method of planting.

1. Genera that do not remain in the ground during the winter and are therefore planted in spring and lifted up in the autumn. These include mainly the garden varieties of gladiolus and tigridia, sometimes also *Crocosmia crocosmiiflora*.

2. Genera that are hardy flower early in spring and are therefore planted in autumn. They may be left undisturbed for a number of years but in the second and especially ensuing years they tend to lose their vigour. The bulbs separate, in time forming a single clump of plants that produce flowers of increasingly smaller size or none at all, and exhaust the supply of nutrients in the soil. For this reason it is really better to lift the

17

bulbs after flowering and they should certainly not be left in the same site for more than three years. This applies first and foremost to tulips. Only small, species tulips may remain in a single spot for a longer time because their rate of weakening is slower. Even comparatively small species tulip bulbs produce flowers and a profusion of smaller flowers on bulbs that have divided is not unattractive.

Annual lifting is likewise preferable for hyacinths, though they, too, can be left in the same place for up to three years. Also ixia hybrids and Dutch irises do better if they are lifted every year and stored for the summer, then planted out again in late autumn — as late as possible so that the leaves do not develop too much before the colder weather sets in and then suffer damage by frost.

It is very important not to plant the bulbs of these two groups in the same bed all the time but to alternate the arrangements according to the given possibilities. If planted continually in the same spot not only the soil is depleted of nutrients but the plants are increasingly prone to damage by pests and diseases so that in time they degenerate. Suitable previous crops are ones that are not attacked by the same pests and diseases as the plants that come after them. The best precursors of bulbs which are planted in early autumn are plants which can be lifted in time for proper preparation of the soil. According to the experience of Dutch growers, tulips may be planted after hyacinths and narcissi after tulips but never in the reverse order.

3. Genera that remain in the ground for a number of years though after a greater length of time they, too, suffer from lack of nutrients and benefit from being transferred to another site. As a rule such plants are lifted after the top parts have dried and they are stored in a dry place during the summer resting period. They include all members of the *Bulbocodium*, *Camassia*, *Crocus*, *Muscari* and *Narcissus* genera, and sometimes also *Crocosmia*.

4. Genera that are transplanted after a greater number of years because they have become too congested and need to be divided. Frequent transfer is not good for them. On the contrary, in the first years following planting they are not as developed and do not flower as well as later when they have become established in their new location. Most of them must be returned

to the soil soon after lifting. Some do not have a period of complete dormancy; their roots do not die and they must be handled with care. The bulbs are also more tender; they do not have a thick outer coat to protect them from drying out and if they must remain out of the ground for some time, such as during shipment, they should be put in damp wood shavings, sand or peat. These include practically all species of *Lilium* and *Fritillaria*, also *Arum*, *Colchicum*, *Cyclamen*, *Ornithogalum* and *Scilla*, as well as *Anemone blanda*, *Chionodoxa luciliae*, *Eranthis hyemalis*, *Eremurus robustus*, *Galanthus nivalis*, *Leucojum vernum*, *Puschkinia scilloides* and *Trillium grandiflorum*.

Members of the third and fourth group, especially those that require rich soil, should be provided with an addition of compost or at least artificial fertilizer every year.

The time of planting according to these divisions, then, is determined in great part by the time of flowering. Autumn is the time to plant those species that flower early in spring. Some benefit if they are stored as long as possible in summer in a warm dry place and if they are planted at the latest possible date so that in the case of warm autumn weather they do not start to make leaves which might then be damaged by frost. It is desirable that they only put out roots in the autumn and do not begin any top growth. Ixia hybrids and Dutch irises are two plants that are best planted as late as the second half of November, tulips and hyacinths in the second half of October. Plants that require a longer time to root or else do not start to make leaves prematurely and, on the contrary, are less hardy if planted later in the year should be put out in the first half of October at the latest. These include all members of *Allium*, *Anemone*, *Arum*, *Bulbocodium*, *Camassia*, *Chionodoxa*, *Eranthis*, *Ornithogalum*, *Puschkinia*, as well as *Iris reticulata* and all species of *Crocus* and *Cyclamen* that flower in spring (those that flower in autumn must be planted in August at the latest). The genus *Muscari* is also planted at the beginning of October. Muscari often start to make leaves in autumn but these are not damaged by frost. September, and better still August, is the time to plant *Narcissus* and *Erythronium* as well as *Eremurus* and *Trillium*. All these genera are easily damaged by frost when planted late in the year and require a heavier cover in winter. August is the time for planting *Colchicum*, which flowers shortly after in

September and should not be stored for a long period. *Leucojum vernum*, *Galanthus nivalis*, *Scilla* and *Fritillaria* should also not be stored long. They are usually planted in August. The best time for transferring lilies is the first half of September when the bulbs are dormant. New bulbs should be planted or transferred as quickly as possible for they have no protection against drying out, their roots are persistent and are not likely to be replaced by new ones if they dry up.

Spring is the time for planting all garden varieties of gladiolus. The offsets or cormlets should be put out as soon as possible, at the end of March if the weather permits, because they generally grow very slowly. Mature corms should be planted at the end of April. This is also the time for planting *Tigridia pavonia*.

The depth at which bulbs and tubers are planted depends largely on their size; a suitable depth for tulips is about $4\,^1/_2$ in., for narcissi about 6 in. Small bulbs and tubers are always planted at a shallower depth than large ones of the same species. It also depends on the requirements of the given species, which show marked variation, but some bulbs will adjust themselves to their most suitable depth, especially if planted too shallowly. New bulbs sometimes grow on stolons thereby putting some distance between themselves and the parent bulb not only in the horizontal but also in the vertical direction, that is, downwards. This is especially true of certain species tulips, which thus make their way to depths of more than 8 in.

Similarly, the bulbs of lilies adjust themselves to suitable depths in loose soil by contracting the basal roots. For lilies, planting at too great a depth is more damaging than shallow planting, for then the bulbs do not have enough air. In heavy soils they should be planted at a shallower depth and in light, sandy soils at a greater depth.

When planting globose or flattened tubers that are dormant and have neither roots nor top parts, care should be taken to place them roots downward and tip upward. If planted the other way around their development will be slower and less uniform and the plants will often be weaker. Bulbs and tubers of those species that do not pass through a period of complete rest and have roots when planted must be put out with great care. Before planting, the bulb and roots should be cleaned, all rotting parts removed and damaged parts treated with flowers of sulphur. The roots should then be carefully spread out over the bottom of the planting hole or furrow and uniformly covered with prepared soil.

Planting in Beds

In gardens, bulbs are planted in beds, in groups either by themselves or together with other flowers, in grass and in front of shrubs. In decorative, geometric beds they are usually planted in rows spaced according to the size of the plant and thereby often the size of the bulb or tuber. The distance between rows should be such as to provide enough room for general care with hand tools and implements. Bulbs may be planted closer together but when this is done one must watch closely for diseased plants and remove them immediately, for under such conditions disease would spread rapidly. For example, medium-large bulbs, that is those of 4 to 5 in. in circumference, should be planted at least 3 in. apart in rows spaced 4 to 6 in. apart. This is a suitable distance for bulbs that are lifted every year. In principle, the distance between bulbs should not be less than three times their diameter.

Care of Newly Planted Bulbs and Tubers

After the bulbs have been planted and the soil lightly tamped down it should be thoroughly watered so that it settles firmly round the bulbs and so that they will have enough moisture to produce roots before the first frosts. Bulbs and tubers that are planted too late are less hardy and must always be provided with a cover, particularly where it is not certain that there will be an adequate snowfall in winter. Fir boughs, leaves or peat are all suitable for this purpose. The bulbs should be covered before the first frosts and the cover removed in spring before they begin to put out leaves. In locations where mice are frequent it is recommended to place small mounds of a suitable pesticide under the cover, mainly next to crocuses of which they are particularly fond. When using such chemicals, it is important to follow the manufacturer's instructions very carefully.

Feeding and Watering

Soil may be improved by the addition of well-rotted compost or manure and, of course, compound fertilizers containing all the essential nutrients of nitrogen, phosphorus and potassium as well as trace elements can also be used. Compound fertilizers are added to the soil in the autumn. In the case of fertilizers containing only one element it is best to add those with phosphorus and potassium in the autumn and nitrogenous fertilizers in early spring, as soon as the ground has thawed — preferably in two small doses.

Watering is generally unnecessary in spring as the ground is adequately supplied with moisture after the winter. Should the spring be a dry one, however, then watering is a must. It is best to water the ground thoroughly so that the moisture reaches the roots rather than in small quantities which only dampen the surface. Some plants, especially lilies, are intolerant of frequent watering of the leaves for then they are more prone to botrytis, most serious of the fungus diseases that attack tulips and lilies. It is therefore recommended to water only the roots. Lilies also benefit from a covering of peat or leaf mould that keeps the ground from drying out, in which case watering may be reduced. The cover should be removed at the end of the summer to permit the soil to dry out in the autumn. Most bulbs are watered until they flower (after the flowering period only in the case of exceptionally dry weather); then the supply of water is greatly limited so that the bulbs may ripen well. In the case of late-flowering species this is especially important for their survival in winter, both if they remain in the ground or are lifted up and stored. Bulbs and tubers that are not ripe or have been lifted up in wet weather are more often prey to fungus diseases which then spread when they are stored.

Protective Sprays and Care of Planted Flowers

A check must be kept on the condition of the plants as soon as they put out leaves in spring. Those that develop late are often diseased and are best removed to prevent spread of the disease. This is a must, for example, in the case of tulips, crocuses, lilies, daffodils and gladioli. A similar check should be made before every spraying with preventive agents.

Species prone to fungus diseases should be sprayed preventively with fungicides, generally against the two most prevalent diseases — botrytis and basal rot caused by *Fusarium* sp. — which attack chiefly tulips, lilies and gladioli. In damp weather spraying should be repeated at least every two weeks, in dry weather and if the plants are in good condition less frequently. In any case, however, tulips, for instance, should be sprayed at least twice before the flowering period and at least once after the flowers have faded. In summer, in the case of tulips generally after the flowering period, plants are treated with a spray combining both fungicide and insecticide, mostly against aphids.

Further care consists of hoeing and weeding. The earth should be hoed as often as necessary to keep it from forming a crust, in which case weeding is usually no problem as the small weeds are destroyed by the hoeing. Nowadays, increasing use is being made of chemical agents — herbicides — to destroy weeds and large-scale cultivation is practically impossible without them. In small plots, however, they must be applied with great care. The given agent must not come in contact with those plants for which it is not intended for the effect might be toxic. The effect and influence of herbicides on the plants is also determined by the condition of the soil. The effect is greater if there is more moisture in the soil but the danger of damage to plants is also greater. If the soil is rich in humus or if it is a clay soil the effect is weaker but the treated plants may still be damaged. Herbicides, therefore, must be applied strictly according to the instructions on the label. In the case of bulbs they are usually applied in spring before the leaves appear or in the autumn after the top parts of the plant have died down.

Certain tall species of bulbs, above all lilies, require some kind of support as the stem is generally too weak to bear the weight of the flowers and might bend or break. It is wise to keep this in mind when planting and to insert a peg beside the bulb. This may later be replaced by a stouter and longer stake without incurring any damage to the bulb. The stem is then tied loosely to the stake at several points.

The most important thing in the garden is a wealth of flowers which one can take delight in for as long as possible. In large-scale horticultural establishments the first concern is the growth of healthy bulbs and tubers. If production of bulbs and tubers is the prime object then the flower or inflorescence is usually removed when the flowering period begins to reach its peak. Pollination and ripening of the ovary, which would weaken the bulb, is thus prevented. (Sometimes the flower is allowed to attain its full bloom but in such a case it is only for the purpose of checking the purity of the species or variety.) The plant is therefore forced to concentrate all the nutrients into the bulb or tuber, the outcome being far greater increase in size and strength. However, even in the small garden it is not a good idea to leave faded flowers on the stalk. Not only are they an unattractive sight but here, too, it is important to have strong, healthy bulbs and tubers for the following year. Besides, fallen petals are often attacked by botrytis. It is not necessary to remove the flowers or inflorescence of small bulbs nor in those parts of the wild garden where one desires to have certain species spread freely by seeding or if one wishes to propagate some from the seed. However, one must always remove the flowers of tulips, gladioli and hyacinths as soon as they have faded. They should be cut or better still broken off (a knife may be instrumental in spreading certain virus diseases) just below the last flower. In the case of hyacinths the flower stalk is left intact and only the individual flowers are plucked. Wherever flowers are used for home decoration and are cut together with the stalk, and especially together with the leaves, the bulb is so weakened that it will not bear flowers or, if it does, very weak ones the following season. Bulbs that suffer most are tulips which have leaves on the stalks and if they are to be long enough to put in a vase generally have to be cut with two leaves. When growing tulips for cutting, therefore, it is best to replace them every year with newly purchased bulbs. Gladioli, likewise, produce few cormlets if raised for cutting and if it is desired to increase a given variety it should be cut just below the last flower. Daffodils do not suffer unduly from cutting; their stalks are leafless and thus there is not such a great loss of the surface area required for photosynthesis.

Lifting Bulbs and Tubers

Tulips, especially in beds, are not at all attractive after they have faded and the bulbs are ripening. If the bed is to look nice and orderly the bulbs should be lifted after the flowers have faded and other flowers planted in their stead. If lifted too soon, however, the bulbs become worthless for they cannot be used again the following year and it is necessary to buy new ones. There is also no sense in leaving the bulbs in the ground and removing only the top parts, for the following season the plants would be weak and non-uniform.

In propagating beds and wherever the bulbs can be left to ripen they should be lifted when the top parts have dried to a greater extent. In the case of tulips they should not be allowed to dry entirely for by then the outer coat of the bulb has completely disintegrated and the individual bulblets fall out when it is lifted, some remaining in the ground and spreading to an unwelcome extent. These bulblets are not destroyed even by deep cultivation (a tulip can grow and flower even if planted at a depth of more then 20 in.). On the other hand, if lifted too soon the bulb is not sufficiently ripe. As a general rule tulip bulbs should be lifted from the second half of June (depending on whether they are early or late-flowering varieties) until about the middle of July. Hyacinths are also lifted at about the same time and daffodils and crocuses, too, if this is necessary. Again, the bulbs should be lifted before the top parts have completely dried. The best time to start is when the leaves begin to wilt and turn yellow at the tip. Daffodils put out new roots very soon and thus should be lifted before this happens. New roots would dry out even if stored for a short time in summer and would be only partially replaced by others. If the plant has few roots it is provided with inadequate nourishment and thus the increase in size and strength is small, besides which there is greater danger of damage by frost.

Bulbs in the small garden are lifted with a spade or flat-tined fork. They should not be left exposed to the sun but should be protected by light shade. In the case of tulips the top parts should be removed as soon as the plants are lifted and the bulbs spread out in frames or boxes in thin layers and stored in a warm, dry room. After they have dried they should be cleaned and divided

25

according to size. The same applies to hyacinths. In the case of daffodils and crocuses the top parts should never be removed forcibly; if they do not come loose easily they should be left and then removed when cleaning the bulbs. Bulbs and tubers should be cleaned shortly after they have dried. Daffodils, in particular, should be made ready for planting early. When cleaning daffodil bulbs the bulblets should never be separated by force, the same applying to the old root remnants. Daffodils should be stored out of doors under a roof-like shelter in a shaded spot. In horticultural establishments tulips and hyacinths are stored in temperature-controlled store rooms; in the home at least in a dry, cool room.

Gladioli must likewise be lifted in time, usually in the first half of October. If lifted later there is increased danger that disease spores present on the leaves during the growing period will make their way to the corms and in winter will spread to other stored corms. Fungus diseases and virus infections sometimes cause great losses in storage.

After lifting the corms, the surrounding soil should be shaken away and the top growth cut off just above the corms, which are then spread out in an airy place to dry. After they have been dried the corms should be cleaned, the remaining top parts broken off, the offsets or spawn separated from the corm and both the corms and offsets stored for the winter in a dry room at a temperature of 43 to 50°F. (6 to 10°C.).

In the summer months, stored bulbs, especially tulips, may be attacked by aphids which spread virus diseases. In such a case the storage space must be fumigated once a week with a suitable insecticide until they are all killed. If mould appears on the stored bulbs it is because they have been dried insufficiently or the air in the store room has a high relative humidity. This can be put right by better ventilation. Bulbs only slightly mouldy on the surface may be planted out. Ones that have become calcified or are covered with large brown hollow spots must be discarded.

Propagation

Bulbous and tuberous plants may be multiplied sexually, that is by means of seeds, or asexually, by vegetative means — parts of the plant, generally of the bulbs or tubers.

Propagation by Means of Seeds

This method is not generally used for increasing bulbs, chiefly because it takes three to seven years to grow a mature plant from the seed, the length of time depending on the species. In the garden, where conditions are quite different from their native habitats, many wild species do not produce any seeds or else the seeds have poor powers of germination. Garden varieties are mostly hybrids so that their offspring show great diversity and sometimes they are even sterile. The last and perhaps main reason for the limited use of this method is that most species form numerous offsets of the bulb or tuber and these develop into mature plants often in the very first year and if not, then within three years at the most. Also the plants are true to type, that is they have the same colour, height, flowering period and other properties.

Bulbous plants produce a fairly large quantity of seed. For example, the capsule of a tulip contains some three hundred seeds, occasionally even more, at least half of which will germinate. Some species have seeds with good powers of germination in open ground. Such plants spread freely in the garden through self-seeding, sometimes even to such an extent that they become a nuisance. This may be prevented, especially in the rock garden where they would destroy more valuable plants, by removing the flowers as soon as they have faded. On the other hand, in the wild garden and in grass such spreading is welcomed for the resulting masses of flowers have a natural look and are very attractive. Bulbs that frequently spread in this way include *Muscari botryoides*, *Scilla hispanica* and *S. sibirica*, sometimes *Chionodoxa luciliae* and *Puschkinia scilloides*, and in suitable locations *Galanthus nivalis*, *Leucojum vernum* and certain species of crocus.

Seeds should be sown in a box or frame as soon as they are ripe or else in the autumn or spring as required. They usually germinate in spring; only in some instances does germination take place later, for instance some lilies do not germinate until the following year. The seeds of most bulbs require a period of cold to germinate uniformly and this is why they are sown in the autumn. They should be protected against damage by frost but left at least several weeks at temperatures slightly above freezing point, for example the best temperature for tulips is about 41°F. (5°C.). During the growing period they should be supplied with adequate moisture and the soil kept clean and loose. During the dormant period seedlings are best kept in drier soil. Very small bulbs should be left in the ground the first and sometimes even the second year; not till the following year should they be lifted and replanted in carefully prepared soil. It is best if they can be grown in frames for at least the first three years. After that the bulbs and tubers may be cultivated in the same way as those obtained by vegetative propagation.

Bulbs propagated in practice by means of seeds include certain species of lilies, *Lilium callosum*, *L. formosanum*, *L. philippinense* and *L. pumilum*, and often *Allium moly*, *Anemone coronaria*, *Arum italicum*, *Camassia cusickii*, *Chionodoxa luciliae*, *Crocosmia crocosmiiflora*, *Eremurus robustus*, *Erythronium dens-canis*, *Eucomis comosa*, *Fritillaria meleagris*, *Leucojum vernum*, *Muscari armeniacum*, *Puschkinia scilloides*, *Scilla sibirica*, *Tigridia pavonia*, type species of crocus and of tulips, for example *Tulipa greigii* and *T. sprengeri*. *Cyclamen europaeum*, whose seedlings take one year to develop and flower the following season, is propagated almost only by means of seeds.

Seeds are also used to grow new varieties. Growing a new variety of tulip, daffodil or gladiolus is a difficult and lengthy task for the first flower-bearing plants are not obtained until the fifth or sixth year and only afterwards, when the seedlings have grown into fully mature plants, is it possible to begin evaluating clones from the aesthetic and grower's viewpoint. This process, during which the clone is multiplied by vegetative propagation, likewise takes a number of years so that it often takes as many as twenty years before a clone is put on the market as a new variety. Species or varieties that have the characters desired in the hybrid are the ones which are selected for crossing. To prevent accidental pollination the plants are isolated and pollinated artificially. The resulting seed is then sown and carefully tended. Even with the best of results the number of seedlings exhibiting only the good features of both parents is very small. To grow a clone that excels existing varieties in some way is not easy, for the number of existing varieties already runs into tens of thousands. It is very difficult to raise forms of new and different hues. A far greater range of opportunities is open to those growers who focus on other characteristics such as long and firm stems, perfection of shape, size and, above all, longevity of flowers, and in the case of gladioli the density and arrangement of the inflorescence as well as fresh, attractive leaves. Most important from the grower's viewpoint is the bulb's power of propagation, resistance to diseases and suitability for forcing.

Vegetative Propagation

Vegetative propagation yields fewer offspring than propagation from seed but they are quicker to develop and cultivation is often easier. Indeed, this is the only way to increase most garden varieties if they are to come true to type. The most common method of vegetative propagation is by means of offsets of the bulb or tuber, or in some tuberous plants by cutting up the tuber. Lilies form comparatively few offsets and thus are frequently propagated by detaching and planting individual bulb scales. There are also species that can be propagated by means of bulbils that form in the axils of the leaves or in certain species of allium in the inflorescence.

Vegetative Propagation of Tulips

Bulb offsets are usually formed spontaneously but sometimes it is necessary to stimulate the process artificially. The number and size of the offsets varies greatly according to genus, species and variety. To a certain extent their formation may be influenced by proper nourishment and storage techniques. Thus, for example, a single mature tulip bulb will produce two to six new bulblets, depending on the species and variety. The old tulip bulb dies after flowering and so all the remaining bulbs are newly formed. The largest new mother bulb is formed in the centre next to the growing point; other increasingly smaller bulblets are formed between the growing point and the outer tunic. The size and number of these offsets may be greatly influenced by the temperature during storage. Higher temperatures promote the growth of a greater number of smaller bulblets whereas lower temperatures yield fewer but larger ones. The temperature also influences the period of flowering and therefore bulbs intended for propagation are stored under different conditions to those intended for planting or forcing. Bulbs of the best class measure more than 12 cm. in circumference. Bulbs with a circumference of less than 10 cm. are for propagation; as a rule they will not produce flowers and require one to two years to attain flowering size. 8 to 10 cm. bulbs may still be planted out in the garden but smaller ones should be put in a propagating bed. Bulbs with a circumference of less than 3 cm. should be discarded; however, this does not apply to small type species.

Vegetative Propagation of Daffodils

Daffodils also produce offsets spontaneously. These take one to three years to develop. The class of daffodil bulbs is determined by the number of joined bulbs. A Class I bulb must be triple, that is composed of three bulbs contained either loosely or firmly within a single cover; a Class II bulb must be double, and a Class III bulb single.

It should be noted that one to two years are similarly required for the development of the bulbs or tubers of *Allium moly*, *Anemone coronaria*, *Arum italicum*, *Camassia cusickii*, *Chionodoxa luciliae*, *Colchicum autumnale*, *Crocosmia crocosmiiflora*, *Crocus chrysanthus*, *Galanthus nivalis*, *Iris hollandica*, *I. reticulata*, *Leucojum vernum*, *Muscari armeniacum*, *Ornithogalum umbellatum*, *Puschkinia scilloides*, *Scilla sibirica* and *Tigridia pavonia*. Offsets of *Fritillaria imperialis* usually take three years to develop.

Vegetative Propagation of Gladioli

Each gladiolus corm forms at least one new corm and often a large number of small cormlets, called spawn, at its base. Often, large corms divide into two to four and sometimes even more corms. The number and size of the cormlets depend in large measure on the variety and also on the feeding of the corm. Cormlets are divided according to their diameter into two classes: Class I — more than 5 mm. across and Class II — less than 5 mm. across. Gladioli can be increased fairly rapidly by means of cormlets. A large cormlet with good powers of growth can produce flowers the same year, though they will be borne late and the spike will be short. Some varieties do not produce enough spawn and so they are sometimes increased by division of the corm. This should be done by cutting it vertically into two or more parts, always leaving a young root at the base and a bud capable of growth at the top of each piece. Corms should be cut shortly before planting and the cut edges allowed to dry. This method of multiplying gladioli is used only by amateur gardeners and is not suitable for the large-scale nurseryman.

Vegetative Propagation of Trilliums and Eremuri

August is a suitable month for propagating trilliums by dividing the rhizomes. This is also the time for dividing clumps of eremurus. Only established crowns which have formed several buds are divided so that at least one bud is found on each part. The incisions are dusted with flowers of sulphur before replanting.

Vegetative Propagation of Hyacinths

Hyacinths are propagated only by large establishments which have the necessary equipment. A hyacinth bulb practically never forms offsets. This occurs only in exceptional cases in very old bulbs (hyacinth bulbs are persistent) or if the basal plate is damaged. A plant with a damaged growing point, which forms at the top of the basal plate, cannot produce flowers nor continue normal growth and thus all food reserves stored in the bulb coats are used by the plant to form substitute growing points, in other words, offsets. This fact has been made use of by growers to stimulate the plant to produce offsets. There are two methods of 'damaging' the growing point, either by removing the root base with a conical incision, thus cutting out the entire basal plate, or else deep incisions are made crosswise or in the shape of a star on the base of the bulb. In either case the cut must reach all the tunic coats. Only bulbs with a circumference of more then 18 cm. are suitable for this purpose. The first method, cutting out the root base, yields numerous small bulblets, whereas cross-cutting yields fewer but larger bulblets. The incisions should be sprinkled with flowers of sulphur and the cut bulb placed in a propagating chamber with a temperature of 80°F. (26°C.) and relative humidity of 80 to 90 per cent., where they are left until time for planting, which should be as late as possible. During this period small bulblets form at the edges of the incisions between the individual coats and these are then set out in the autumn together with the parent bulb (without being separated from it) in well-prepared soil. Late planting is important in that the longer the incubation period the larger the bulblets. The beds in which they are set out should be covered with fir boughs or peat before the onset of winter frosts. During the growing period the old bulb dies and the released bulblets are lifted in June and further cultivated, it taking at least three years for them to develop. Only wild species hyacinths multiply either spontaneously or produce an adequate number of seeds with good powers of germination.

Propagation of Lilies

The propagation of lilies requires to be dealt with in some detail. Many species are often increased by means of seeds, which germinate in two different ways, depending on the species. Either the cotyledon grows up above the ground, which is known as epigeal germination, or else it remains below the ground while a small bulb is formed from which the true leaf grows the following year; this is called hypogeal germination. For those who wish to grow lilies from seed this differentiation is important and they must be fully aware of it so as not to be misled into thinking that the seeds of the second group lack the power of germination.

Vegetative methods of increase include division of the bulbs, that is separation of bulbs growing at the side and above the mother bulb. This method, however, is very slow. A better way is by means of bulbils which form up the stem in the axils of the leaves; they are produced, however, by only a few species. Bulbils should be detached when they are sufficiently ripe and are beginning to come loose. They should be planted at a depth of about ¾ in. in a frame or in well-prepared beds where, as a rule, they soon put out roots; some species even put out leaves in the same year whereas others do not begin to grow until spring. Bulbils are formed primarily by *L. bulbiferum*, *L. sargentiae* and *L. tigrinum*, sometimes, though rarely, also by species which normally do not bear them.

The most frequent method of vegetative propagation is by means of bulb scales; as many as one third of the scales may be removed from a strong and healthy bulb. Scales should be detached together with their base for it is there that new bulbs are formed. They are generally detached in the autumn when bulbs are being transplanted, even though according to the experience of lily raisers, bulbs grow best from scales removed during the flowering period. However, for the amateur gardener who only wishes to remove a small number of scales, the easiest method is to leave the bulb in the ground, draw back some soil and carefully break the scales off. After treating the wounds with flowers of sulphur, the bulb is covered again with soil. The point of separation on the scales should also be dusted with flowers of sulphur. The scales should then be placed tip upwards in boxes filled with a propagating mixture and put in a propagating frame with a temperature of 65 to 68°F. (18 to 20°C.). The rate of development varies according to the species. The fastest growing lilies, for instance, are the Mid Century Hybrids and the ones with the slowest rate of growth are *L. speciosum* and *L. auratum*.

Classification of Garden Varieties

Inasmuch as some 10,000 forms of tulips, a like number of daffodils and lilies and some 100,000 forms of gladioli have been developed through selection and breeding it is impossible to get along without some kind of classification into groups that would allow comparison of individual varieties with similar characteristics. Varieties are divided according to colour, shape of the flower, height, period of flowering and parentage or origin. Division according to colour is used in all genera and species which occur in several colours and where, in view of the comparatively limited number of varieties, this classification suffices. It is inadequate, however, for tulips, gladioli, lilies and especially daffodils, where division according to colour may be used only in subgroups. These bulbs are listed according to official international classifications even in catalogues and it is therefore useful to know them. The classification of garden varieties has nothing in common with the botanical classification of the typical species, which are generally listed separately.

Daffodils

Narcissi are grouped into twelve divisions, mainly according to the shape of the flower.

DIVISION I.   Trumpet narcissi. This section includes all varieties that have one flower to a stem and trumpet or corona as long as or longer than the perianth segments. They are divided according to colour into four subdivisions:

a) Varieties with perianth and corona coloured, usually yellow.
b) Varieties with perianth white or near white and corona coloured.
c) Varieties with perianth and corona white, the latter not paler than the perianth.
d) Varieties not falling into any of the preceding categories (a, b or c). One such example is Spellbinder with perianth yellow and corona white.

DIVISION II.   Large-cupped narcissi. This section includes

varieties that likewise have only one flower to a stem, the corona more than one-third but less than equal to the length of the perianth segments. They are divided into four subdivisions in like manner to the trumpet narcissi.

DIVISION III. Small-cupped narcissi. This section includes varieties that also have just one flower to a stem, the corona not more than one-third the length of the perianth segments. They are divided into four subdivisions the same as in Divisions I and II.

DIVISION IV. Double narcissi. This section embraces all double varieties, including multiflowered ones which were previously classed in Division VIII (Tazetta narcissi) or other divisions.

DIVISION V. Triandrus narcissi. This section includes all varieties that are clearly descended from *Narcissus triandrus*. They generally have two to three flowers and are divided into two subdivisions according to the length of the corona:

a) Corona not less than two-thirds the length of the perianth segments.

b) Corona less then two-thirds the length of the perianth segments.

DIVISION VI. Cyclamineus narcissi. This section includes all varieties that are clearly descended from *Narcissus cyclamineus*. They are divided into two subdivisions according to the length of the corona, the same as those of the Triandrus division.

DIVISION VII. Jonquilla narcissi. This section includes all varieties that are clearly descended from *Narcissus jonquilla*. They, too, are divided into two subdivisions the same as Divisions V and VI.

DIVISION VIII. Tazetta narcissi. Varieties that are clearly descended from *Narcissus tazetta*; they are all multiflowered.

DIVISION IX. Poeticus narcissi. This section includes all *Narcissus poeticus* hybrids that have retained the essential characteristics of the species.

DIVISION X. Type species and their hybrids.

DIVISION XI. Narcissi with divided corona. This is a new section embracing varieties with corona divided into segments at least one-third of its length.

DIVISION XII. Various other narcissi that do not fall into any of the preceding divisions.

Tulips

Tulips are divided into fifteen groups according to their flowering period, shape of the flower and other characteristics.

Early-flowering tulips:
DIVISION I. Single early tulips. Small varieties generally used for forcing in pots, only rarely for planting out.
DIVISION II. Double early tulips. Small varieties with double flowers, likewise used mainly for forcing in pots, sometimes also for planting out.

Mid-season tulips:
DIVISION III. Mendel tulips. Varieties of medium height resulting from crosses between Duc van Tol and Darwin varieties. They are used for forcing for cutting, less commonly for bedding.
DIVISION IV. Triumph tulips. Varieties of medium height resulting from crosses between single early-flowering tulips and single late-flowering varieties. They flower somewhat later than the Mendel tulips, are more robust and have a stouter stem. For this reason they are very good for cutting and most varieties are also suitable for forcing for cutting. This group is one of the most important.
DIVISION V. Darwin hybrids. This is the most recent group of tulips established for varieties resulting from crosses between the Darwin tulips and *Tulipa fosteriana*, all with essential characteristics clearly indicating their parentage. Compared with the Darwin tulips they flowered earlier, were larger and more vigorous but not as longlived and in most cases the colour was a glowing scarlet-red. In recent years other varieties resulting from crosses with species tulips have been added to this group. All are distinguished by their large size and stout stems, are usually easy to propagate and flower fairly early. Their one disadvantage is that the flowers open wide soon after cutting.

Late-flowering tulips:
DIVISION VI. Darwin tulips. This group embraces the greatest number of varieties. All are tall with stout stems and

firm flowers that have a typical angular shape, almost rectangular in cross-section, and great longevity in the vase. They are almost always a single glowing colour; two-coloured forms are rare. During the most recent changes in the classification of tulips the majority of Breeder tulips were added to this group, a few being relegated to the Cottage tulip division. Breeder tulips are very old and very late-flowering varieties distinguished from the Darwin varieties chiefly by their soft smoky colours, frequently combined with orange, red or brown with various shades of mauve. These varieties are rarely cultivated nowadays because they flower late and are not suitable for forcing. Darwin and Breeder tulips are mostly good for planting out and for cutting. Some Darwin tulips are excellent for forcing.

DIVISION VII. Lily-flowered tulips. These are distinguished by the long, narrow, pointed petals. They are relatively late-flowering and are suitable primarily for cutting.

DIVISION VIII. Cottage tulips (Single late tulips). All late-flowering varieties with shape of flower that does not fit into either of the two preceding groups (Division VI or VII). They therefore do not have more precise unifying characteristics. The flowers are usually oval but the group embraces also the Viridiflora tulips with green flowers resembling the open blooms of the lily-flowered tulips. This section also includes all multi-flowered garden varieties.

DIVISION IX. Rembrandt tulips. This is an old group embracing varieties with flowers with flame-like markings, striped brown, bronze, black, reddish-pink or purple on a red, white or yellow ground. It includes the former Rembrandt, Bizarre and Bybloemen tulips.

DIVISION X. Parrot tulips. Varieties with pointed, fringed or laciniate petals. All parrot tulips have developed spontaneously as mutations; no grower has as yet succeeded in cultivating them by crossing. Parrot tulips are suitable for cutting and for planting out, but old forms, unfortunately, tend to have a stem too weak for the heavy flower and therefore are bent to the ground by rain and wind.

DIVISION XI. Double late tulips. These are distinguished from the double early tulips by their later flowering, greater height and more compact flowers. The lengthier stems make them not only good garden plants but also good for cutting.

37

Species tulips:

DIVISION XII. Kaufmanniana hybrids and varieties. These are very early-flowering species tulips, crosses with *Tulipa greigii* often having blotched or streaked leaves. They are small (in some the stem is not even 4 in. high) and therefore suitable only for planting out.

DIVISION XIII. Fosteriana hybrids and varieties. These are early-flowering tulips with large flowers and are generally more robust and taller than *Tulipa kaufmanniana*. Some hybrids have the leaves spotted or striped brownish-purple. They are suitable mainly for planting out, certain taller forms also for cutting, though they do not last long in the vase.

DIVISION XIV. Greigii hybrids and varieties. All hybrids and varieties have markings on the leaves. They flower later than *Tulipa kaufmanniana* tulips and generally later than *T. fosteriana* varieties and are also suitable only for planting out.

DIVISION XV. Other species tulips, their hybrids and varieties. This is a diversified group embracing dwarf, small-flowered and multiflowered species used mainly in the rock garden as well as all tall wild species. Most are early species, flowering before the garden varieties, but some are also very late-flowering, for example *Tulipa sprengeri*. All species tulips are cultivated only as garden plants; some are excellent for the rock garden. They are not suitable for forcing or for cutting because they are not long-lived in the vase.

Lilies

Lilies may be classified according to their geographical origin and parentage, which, unlike other bulbous plants, is known, for the great boom in their breeding and cultivation began only a few decades ago. They may also be classified according to the shape of the flower. Though this, like other arbitrary divisions, is not sufficiently precise, nevertheless it is an important guideline in the vast selection of lily varieties.

When classified by shape, lilies are divided into three groups according to the type of flower. The first is the classic trumpet, which may be widely expanded or very slim with long, narrow petals. The second is the cup-shaped to flat lily, which may even resemble a star. And the third is the Turk's-cap lily with reflexed petals, sometimes curving back to the stem. The most useful classification, however, is the one drawn up by the Royal Horticultural Society and the North American Lily Society, which divides lilies into nine divisions.

DIVISION I. Asiatic hybrids. This section includes hybrids from *Lilium tigrinum*, *L. cernuum*, *L. davidii*, *L. maximowiczii*, *L.* × *maculatum*, *L.* × *hollandicum*, *L. amabile*, *L. pumilum*, *L. concolor* and *L. bulbiferum*.

a) Early-flowering lilies with upright flowers, either single or in umbels, such as 'Enchantment', 'George Jackson', 'Golden Wonder' and 'Joan Evans'.
b) Lilies with outward-facing flowers such as 'Brandywine', 'Fire Flame', 'Prosperity' and 'Valencia'.
c) Lilies with pendant flowers such as 'Citronella', 'Edith Cecilia', 'Lady Bowes Lyon' and 'White Princess'.

DIVISION II. Martagon hybrids. All crosses with either *Lilium martagon* or *L. hansonii* as one of the parents. They include the Backhouse Hybrids and Paisley Strain.

DIVISION III. Hybrids from *Lilium candidum*, *L. chalcedonicum* and other European species, excepting *L. martagon*. They include 'Apollo', *L.* × *testaceum* and 'Zeus'.

DIVISION IV. American hybrids. Only crosses between American species. They include the Bellingham Hybrids, 'Shuksan', the Henry Bolander Hybrids and 'Sir Launcelot'.

DIVISION V. Hybrids that are derived from *Lilium longiflorum* and *L. formosanum*. Examples are *L.* × *formolongii* and 'Formobel'.

DIVISION VI. Hybrids from trumpet lilies and Aurelian hybrids derived from Asiatic species including *Lilium henryi*. Excluded are hybrids from *L. auratum*, *L. speciosum*, *L. japonicum* and *L. rubellum*.

a) Trumpet-shaped lilies. This includes all hybrids with flowers the shape of a trumpet, such as African Queen Strain, 'Black Dragon', Golden Clarion Strain, 'Limelight' and 'Sulphur Queen'.
b) Bowl-shaped lilies. All hybrids with flowers clearly bowl-shaped and facing outward, such as 'Gwendolyn Anley', Heart's Desire Strain and 'New Era'.

c) Lilies with pendant flowers. All hybrids with flowers distinctly pendant, for example, Golden Showers Strain.

d) Sunburst lilies. All forms with flat-opening and star-shaped flowers, for example, 'Bright Star' and Golden Sunburst Strain.

DIVISION VII. Crosses between Far Eastern species such as *Lilium auratum*, *L. speciosum*, *L. japonicum*, *L. rubellum* and their crosses with *L. henryi*.

a) Trumpet-shaped flowers.

b) Bowl-shaped flowers, for example 'Empress of India'.

c) Flat-faced flowers, for example 'Jillian Wallace'.

d) Recurved flowers, for example Jamboree Strain and Potomac Hybrids.

DIVISION VIII. All hybrids that do not fit in any of the preceding sections.

DIVISION IX. All species lilies and their original forms.

a) Martagon forms. All species with Turk's-cap flowers excepting the American species.
   Included here are *Lilium cernuum*, *L. chalcedonicum*, *L. davidii*, *L. duchartrei*, *L. hansonii*, *L. henryi*, *L. martagon*, *L. monadelphum* and *L. wardii*.

b) Species with upright flowers such as *Lilium bulbiferum*, *L. dauricum* and *L. tsingtauense*.

c) American species.

d) Forms of *Lilium formosanum*, *L. longiflorum* and *L. philippinense*.

e) Species with bowl-shaped and trumpet-shaped flowers apart from those that fall into group d. They are *Lilium candidum*, *L. regale*, *L. sargentiae* and *L. sulphureum*.

f) Asiatic lilies with short trumpets or slightly reflexed petals such as *Lilium bakerianum*, *L. nepalense* and *L. primulinum*.

g) Forms and varieties of *Lilium auratum* and *L. speciosum*.

h) Asiatic, generally dwarf lilies that are closely related to the genus *Nomocharis*. They include *Lilium henrici*, *L. mackliniae*, *L. nanum* and *L. sherriffiae*.

Gladioli

Gladioli, with their many well-known and valuable varieties, have a very complex and generally unknown parentage. It is impossible to cover the vast number of varieties bred and raised to date. Their classification, according to a given system, is a task of enormous proportions and that is why there is no firmly established classification as yet. In America varieties are classified according to the size and colour of the flowers by a three-digit numeral, the first digit denoting the size, the second the basic colour and the third the shade or markings.

The temporary classification currently used in Europe divides gladioli into nine basic groups which are further divided according to colour and flowering period. Catalogues often differentiate only large-flowered, small-flowered and species gladioli.

DIVISION I. Species gladioli and their hybrids.

DIVISION II. Early-flowering gladioli (Nanus, Colvillei, Herald, Tubergeni and Harlemensis gladioli).

DIVISION III. Primulinus gladioli and Primulinus hybrids.

DIVISION IV. Small-flowered gladioli (Butterfly, Mignon and Miniature gladioli).

DIVISION V. Large-flowered gladioli.

DIVISION VI. Large-flowered frilled gladioli.

DIVISION VII. Double gladioli.

DIVISION VIII. Orchid gladioli.

DIVISION IX. Scented gladioli.

Other Bulbous Plants

Other genera can usually be divided simply according to colour or some other unifying characteristic. Hyacinths, besides being divided into groups according to colour, also include a separate group of double hyacinths. Crocuses are generally divided into three groups: autumn-flowering species, spring-flowering species and large-flowered garden varieties. Sometimes the *Crocus chrysanthus* hybrids, which are the most numerous, are placed in a separate group.

Uses of Bulbs

Bulbous and tuberous plants may be used in many different ways, though not all species may be planted just anywhere. Before making a selection it is wise to consider where we wish to have the most flowers in early spring and in what part of the garden we want to have the summer- or autumn-flowering plants. One must also take into account that spring bulbs, in particular, have a fairly brief flowering period and some are not attractive after they have faded; it is thus necessary to decide if they are to be lifted at this time, replaced by annuals and in the autumn by new bulbs, or else planted in a location where they will later be concealed by other flowers so that the bulbs may be left in the ground to ripen and then lifted at a suitable time. Although this characteristic of bulbs is to their disadvantage, yet it is unthinkable to have a garden without them. Besides, even other spring perennials do not have a lengthier flowering period than bulbs, whose drawbacks are richly compensated for by their earliness.

Bulbs for Mass Planting

The most widely cultivated bulbous plants are those suitable for mass planting. Hardy, early-flowering bulbs of bright colours are used for this purpose. They are planted chiefly in public parks and large gardens in geometric or asymmetric beds, generally only a single variety to a bed or else a suitable combination of two or three varieties of different colours. Best suited for this purpose are tulips which offer a wide range of choice and whose colour effect makes them practically indispensable in spring.

Invaluable for the wild sections of parks are those species that grow fairly well in grass, especially if, given a favourable location, they seed and spread freely to form attractive masses. These include, for instance, *Muscari armeniacum, Puschkinia scilloides, Scilla campanulata,* certain species of *Allium,* in a suitable situation also *Colchicum autumnale,* certain species of *Crocus,*

Eranthis hyemalis, Erythronium dens-canis and *Ornithogalum umbellatum*, which are sometimes used as a substitute for grass. In damp meadows particularly, *Galanthus nivalis* and *Leucojum vernum* and sometimes also *Bulbocodium vernum*; and near expanses of water, *Fritillaria meleagris*. The most popular bulbs for growing in grass are all the hardier species and varieties of daffodils.

Suitable conditions for more demanding species may be provided in grass by planting them so that they form irregular 'islands' where they can be tended in a similar way to those growing in beds. This form of island planting is also suitable for some tall species which may be planted in small numbers in front of shrubs. These include tall species of *Allium, Eremurus robustus, Eucomis comosa, Fritillaria imperialis* and certain species of lilies.

Bulbs for Mixed Beds

A frequent method of planting bulbs in the garden is in beds of mixed bulbs or beds together with other perennials. This is suitable for those species that have no specific requirements and may be left in the ground for a number of years. If the bulbs are selected wisely such a mixed bed can be attractive throughout the whole growing season. The various species flower successively one after the other and the fresh green foliage of the late-flowering bulbs serves to conceal the faded and drying remains of the early species as their bulbs ripen. Planted together in this manner, for instance, are certain species of *Fritillaria, Muscari* and *Narcissus*, likewise members of the genera *Allium, Camassia, Galtonia, Hyacinthus, Iris* and *Tulipa* and *Anemone coronaria*. Suitable perennials for mixed planting include *Dicentra, Doronicum, Hemerocallis*, certain species of *Primula* and others.

Small bulbs are excellent plants when space is at a premium, and they are often planted in the rock garden or its vicinity. Bulbous plants are not rock garden plants in the true meaning of the term; they cannot be put in poor, gravelly sites between stones, where the bulbs and tubers would have no room to develop. In the wild they are generally found in alpine meadows where they grow even in grass, but always in soil that is rich in humus and is usually moist in spring.

Bulbs for Cutting

Bulbs grown for cutting are those with long stems and adequate longevity in the vase. Bulbs planted in the garden primarily for this purpose should be put in a separate bed at the back of the ornamental garden where the remains of the cut flowers, which are certainly not very attractive, will not be so noticeable. This applies mainly to gladioli, which are grown primarily for cutting, as well as to tulips and irises. Cutting does not spoil the effect of daffodils too much, nor of the small snowdrops, snowflakes or muscari, so these need not be planted separately.

Bulbs for Forcing

The most highly valued aspect of bulbous plants is their use for forcing. Elaborate technological procedures have made it possible for flowering bulbs to be available in shops practically the whole year through. The most important bulbs for this purpose are hyacinths, tulips, Dutch irises and daffodils. Many other small bulbs are used for forcing for early flowering, including crocuses and dwarf irises such as *Iris reticulata*. Of the large-flowered plants, lilies and gladioli are often forced.

When choosing bulbs for early forcing it is best to buy those which have been specially prepared for forcing by thermal treatment. This is especially important if one wants flowers for the Christmas season. These prepared bulbs should be grown according to the directions printed on the container or supplied with the bulbs when purchased. In the case of untreated bulbs, Brilliant Star and Joffre tulips may be used for forcing for Christmas flowering. They should be put in pots and plunged in a bed by the end of August and removed from the bed on December 1st.

In general, bulbs for forcing are best planted in mid-September. They should be put close together in pots, bowls or boxes; hyacinths usually one bulb to a pot or three to a bowl, tulips at least three bulbs together, crocuses five or more to a bowl or pot. Daffodils and tulips intended for cutting are generally planted in boxes filled with a mixture of light, well-drained garden soil and sand. It need not be particularly rich for the plants feed on the food reserves stored in the bulb. Only healthy bulbs and tubers of the largest size are used for forcing. The depth of planting is not the same for all species. Daffodils and hyacinths should be planted with the tip of the bulb above the surface, tulip bulbs should be lightly covered with soil. Crocuses, Dutch irises, muscari, snowdrops and squills should be covered with an inch of soil, and *Iris reticulata* with a 1- to 2-in. layer. After planting, the bulbs should be watered thoroughly and the pots placed close beside each other in a previously prepared bed in a sheltered spot in the garden. The bed should be about 8 in. deep and the bottom covered with a thin layer of sand. The pots and boxes should be covered with about 4 in. of coarse sand or peat and then with an inch or so of soil (more in particularly cold areas). The bed should not be allowed to become too wet in winter. Boxes and pots may also be put in a frame where it is easier to protect them from freezing, but they will still need the covering of peat and soil. In the house, pots may be placed in the dark in a cellar or in a cool room, being watered occasionally so that the bulbs root well. The temperature in the beds where the pots are plunged should not rise above 50°F. (10°C.), otherwise flowering will be delayed. With the onset of the first frosts the beds should be provided with an additional cover of leaves or fir boughs so that the soil surface does not freeze and the bulbs can be lifted in mid-winter. It takes on average ten to twelve weeks for bulbs to root. The quickest to root are prepared hyacinths — six to eight weeks — crocuses take eight weeks, daffodils ten weeks, tulips twelve weeks. Well-rooted bulbs have started to put out leaves and can then be taken into a room in the house, which, however, should not be too warm at first. Crocuses, in particular, do not tolerate temperatures above 50°F. (10°C.). Daffodils should be put in a room with a temperature of 55 to 60°F. (13 to 16°C.) after a few days but hyacinths and tulips require a higher temperature of 65°F. (18°C.). Hyacinths and tulips should be kept in the dark when they are first brought into the warmth. This allows the flower stems to lengthen so that the blooms will be held well above the leaves. After a few days the containers should be moved into full light. This procedure is not necessary in the case of daffodils, which can be moved straight from the plunge bed to a light position. Careful watering is very important with all bulbs.

In the home, hyacinths are often grown in water in special glass containers. The containers should be absolutely clean and only soft water should be used. A piece of charcoal, which serves to prevent decay, is placed inside. The bulb should not be immersed in the water but should be about $\frac{1}{4}$ in. above the surface. Only the roots (as they develop) are submerged. The water may be exchanged every now and then if this can be done without damaging the roots, and as it evaporates, it should be topped up, care being taken not to wet the bulb. The containers should be put in a room with a temperature no higher than 54°F. (12°C.) for a period of eight to ten weeks. Afterwards, transfer them to a cool and later a warm room, but keep the buds in the dark by covering with newspaper until the flower stems have lengthened. This method of forcing may be used up until January. Only the largest bulbs should be used so that the plant has sufficient food reserves for its growth. Prepared bulbs suitable for this purpose are 'Arentine Arendsen', 'Bismarck', 'Jan Bos' and 'Yellow Hammer'.

Uses of the Various Genera

Allium — tall species such as *A. albopilosum*, *A. giganteum* and *A. rosenbachianum* are generally planted in groups in beds of perennials or in grass with other perennials serving to conceal their leaves after they have died, which is very quickly. Some inflorescences are very decorative even after the flowers have faded *(A. albopilosum)*. The small species *A. moly*, *A. oreophilum*, *A. ostrowskianum* and others are best suited for the rock garden, will generally do well in any location and tolerate semi-shade.

Anemone — *A. apennina* and *A. blanda* are planted mostly in the rock garden. *Anemone coronaria* may likewise be planted in the larger rock garden, but is generally put out in beds together with other perennials. It is also a popular bulb for cutting and forcing.

Chionodoxa, Puschkinia and *Scilla* — popular for the rock garden, where they are planted together with other small spring bulbs. They will also grow in grass and semi-shade and will sometimes spread through self-seeding. Taller forms, such as *Scilla hispanica*, are used for cutting.

Colchicum — generally planted in asymmetrical groups in grass, also near the rock garden but only in places where the fairly large leaves, which grow and die at the same time as those of spring bulbs, will not be in the way in spring. Hardy species run wild in suitable locations.

Crocosmia — grown in beds, where it flowers for a comparatively long time. Popular also for cutting.

Crocus — used for forcing in pots and bowls, planting in beds together with other bulbs, frequently in the rock garden, especially species crocus and hybrids. Hardier forms may also be planted in grass, where they sometimes seed and spread freely.

Cyclamen — requires a sheltered and shaded location with plenty of lime in the soil. It is planted in small scattered groups, generally in the rock garden as well as elsewhere under trees and shrubs.

Eranthis — good for planting in grass and in semi-shade as well as in the rock garden. In a suitable location it often seeds and spreads freely.

Erythronium — semi-shade and humus-rich soil are preferred by members of this genus. They are planted in small groups under deciduous trees and shrubs. Sometimes it takes several years for them to become established.

Eucomis and *Eremurus* — almost exotic-looking bulbs which are planted in small groups or singly at the back of perennial beds or in front of groups of taller shrubs. Only species of lesser height are planted in the small garden.

Fritillaria — tall species, above all *F. imperialis*, are planted in small groups, generally at the back of beds of perennials. *Fritillaria meleagris* likewise in smaller groups and also in the rock garden together with other small bulbs, but not in a spot that is too dry; it is also good on the banks of ponds and streams but is rarely used for cutting.

Galanthus and *Leucojum* — these are generally planted in damp locations, in grass and in semi-shade under deciduous trees. They are also grown for cutting.

Galtonia — may be planted in groups in grass and in beds of perennials and is also sometimes used for cutting.

Gladiolus — used primarily for cutting. It is less suitable for ornamental beds because, being planted at a shallow depth, it will not stand up securely and will fall to the ground, especially in damp weather. Beds of gladioli are best located at the back of the ornamental garden for they do not bloom uniformly and when cut present a rather unattractive sight. They are also used commercially for forcing.

Hyacinthus — most commonly used for forcing in pots or bowls. They are also planted in beds, either by themselves or together with other bulbs. They are sometimes planted in smaller groups in grass, but there they tend to be short-lived.

Iris anglica, *I. hispanica* and *I. hollandica (Xiphium)* — these are planted in small groups in beds of perennials, especially *I. anglica*, which is the hardiest. They are excellent for cutting and very valuable for forcing, chiefly *I. hollandica*. Prepared bulbs are used commercially for forcing.

Iris danfordiae and *I. reticulata* — popular rock garden plants along with other members of this group. They are also grown in pots and bowls in the same way as crocuses.

Ixia — planted in beds in small clumps amidst other perennials or in the border. Smaller species also grown in the rock garden. It is excellent for cutting.

Leucojum see *Galanthus*.

Lilium — generally planted in small groups in beds; hardier species also in grass in front of shrubs. When planting lilies it is necessary to keep in mind the requirements of the various species as regards light and the amount of lime in the soil, especially in the case of species lilies. Garden varieties are generally hardier. Lilies are very popular for cutting though a somewhat unpleasant factor is the large quantity of coloured pollen which soils the flowers and the area around the vase. For this reason anthers are sometimes removed, though this, again, detracts from their beauty. Some lilies also have an overpowering scent. The flowers, however, are very long-lived and stand up well to shipping if they are cut when the buds are beginning to colour. Lilies are also used for forcing commercially.

Muscari — most frequently cultivated are the smaller species which are planted as a border to perennial beds, particularly together with daffodils and tulips; sometimes in the rock garden as well as in grass, where they do fairly well. In a favourable position they will seed and spread freely. They are also popular for cutting.

Narcissus — suitable for cutting, forcing and planting in grass, where the common, less demanding varieties may grow and spread for a number of years. Daffodils are rarely planted in beds by themselves; generally they are put out in large groups or in beds together with other bulbs, mainly tulips, hyacinths and muscari. Small species daffodils are also planted near the rock garden and often near water.

Nerine — requires a warm, sunny location and is generally grown in beds, where it is planted in small groups. Frequently cultivated in a cool greenhouse.

Ornithogalum — *O. umbellatum* does well under deciduous trees and is good in the rock garden, where it is planted together with other small bulbs. *Ornithogalum narbonense* and *O. pyramidale* are tall forms, good for planting in small groups in beds of perennials and in grass as well as for cutting. They, too, tolerate semi-shade.

Puschkinia see *Chionodoxa*.

Scilla see *Chionodoxa*.

Tigridia — planted in beds, generally in small groups, together with other summer bulbs such as *Crocosmia crocosmiiflora*, *Galtonia candicans* and the like.

Trillium — suitable only for growing in humus-rich, acid soil and in semi-shade. For this reason it is generally planted in association with shrubs and ferns. It is also forced and sometimes used for cutting.

Tulipa — great numbers are used for forcing, small ones in pots and tall ones in boxes, the latter also being used for cutting. Varieties mostly grown for cutting are tall, late-flowering tulips with stout stems. Cut flowers are easy to pack and stand up well to shipping. In large gardens and parks tulips are planted in beds containing one of a kind, generally small brightly-coloured forms, sometimes also double forms and taller species tulips, primarily *T. fosteriana* and *T. greigii* hybrids, *T. eichleri* and *T. praestans*. Hardier varieties and species tulips may also be planted in grass, a location fairly well tolerated by *T. kaufmanniana* and others, though here they sometimes need to be renewed. Small species tulips are also planted in the rock garden. Suitable for this purpose are *T. batalinii*, *T. maximowiczii*, *T. tarda* and small *T. kaufmanniana* forms. Tulips may also be used in beds of mixed flowers but one disadvantage is that they need to be transplanted more frequently than other bulbs and perennials.

TABLE I.

Bulbs for Planting in Grass

S = sun   s-Sh = semi-shade   Sh = shade   D = damp location

Plant	Conditions	Comments
Allium — most species	S generally	
Arum italicum and other species	s-Sh, Sh, D	
Bulbocodium vernum	S, s-Sh, D	sometimes also runs wild
Colchicum autumnale	S, s-Sh, D	
Colchicum speciosum	S, s-Sh	
Crocus chrysanthus and certain other species	S, s-Sh	some forms run wild
Crocus speciosus and other autumn crocuses	S, s-Sh	
Crocus vernus garden varieties	S, s-Sh	
Endymion hispanicus	S, s-Sh	
Eranthis hyemalis	S, s-Sh	naturalises among shrubs
Fritillaria meleagris	s-Sh	on the banks of ponds
Galanthus nivalis	S, s-Sh	runs wild
Hyacinthella azurea	S, s-Sh, tolerates Sh	runs wild
Hyacinthus amethystinus	S, sometimes s-Sh	
Leucojum vernum	s-Sh, D	runs wild
Muscari — most species	S, s-Sh	runs wild
Narcissus — hardy species and varieties	S, in rare cases s-Sh	often beside expanses of water
Ornithogalum umbellatum	S, s-Sh	runs wild
Puschkinia scilloides	S, s-Sh	
Scilla pratensis	S, s-Sh	runs wild
Scilla sibirica	S, s-Sh	runs wild
Tulipa kaufmanniana and other hardy species and varieties	S	
Tulipa tarda	S	

TABLE II.

Bulbs for the Mixed Bed

S = sun   s-Sh = semi-shade   Sh = shade   D = damp location

Plant	Conditions	Height
Allium — all taller species	S	medium to tall
Anemone coronaria	S	medium
Camassia — all species	S	medium to tall
Crocosmia crocosmiiflora	S	medium
Endymion hispanicus	S, s-Sh	medium
Fritillaria imperialis	S	tall
Fritillaria meleagris	S, s-Sh	medium
Galtonia candicans	S	medium to tall
Gladiolus — type species	S	medium
Hyacinthella azurea	S, s-Sh	small
Hyacinthus amethystinus	S	small
Hyacinthus - garden varieties	S	small to medium
Iris anglica	S, s-Sh	medium
Ixia hybrids	S, s-Sh	medium
Lilium — hardier species and varieties	S, s-Sh	medium to tall
Muscari — all species	S, s-Sh	small and medium
Narcissus — most strong-growing species and varieties	S, in rare cases s-Sh	medium
Ornithogalum narbonense	s-Sh	medium
Ornithogalum pyramidale	s-Sh	medium
Tulipa — all taller species and varieties	S	medium

TABLE III.

Bulbs for the Rock Garden

S = sun   s-Sh = semi-shade   Sh = shade   D = damp location

Plant	Conditions	Comments
Allium — all small species (*A. karataviense*, *A. moly*, *A. neapolitanum* and *A. ostrowskianum*)		
Anemone apennina, *A. blanda*	S, s-Sh	
Anemone coronaria		only for larger rock gardens
Bulbocodium vernum		
Chionodoxa luciliae	s-Sh	
Crocus — all species and varieties		
Cyclamen — all species	s-Sh, lime	
Eranthis hyemalis		
Erythronium — all species	s-Sh	loose, humus-rich soil
Fritillaria meleagris		mainly at the edge of rock gardens where soil is deep and loose
Galanthus nivalis		only at the edge of rock gardens
Hyacinthella azurea		
Hyacinthus amethystinus		
Iris reticulata		
Leucojum vernum		only at the edge of rock gardens
Muscari — all small species		
Narcissus — hardier, small type species		depending on the species, some in a damp location
Ornithogalum umbellatum		loose, humus-rich soil
Puschkinia scilloides		
Scilla — all species		

TABLE III. (continued)

Plant	Conditions	Comments
Trillium grandiflorum	s-Sh, acid soil	only in larger rock gardens or their vicinity
Tulipa — all small species (*T. batalinii, T. chrysantha, T. clusiana*, small *T. greigii* hybrids, *T. hageri, T. humilis, T. kaufmanniana, T. kolpakowskiana, T. linifolia, T. maximowiczii, T. orphanidea, T. suaveolens, T. tarda, T. turkestanica, T. urumiensis* and *T. violacea*)		

TABLE IV.

Bulbs for Cutting

Allium — all taller species	
Anemone coronaria	
Camassia — all species	
Crocosmia crocosmiiflora	
Endymion hispanicus	
Galanthus nivalis	occasionally
Galtonia candicans	
Gladiolus — all varieties	grown mainly for cutting
Hyacinthella azurea	occasionally
Hyacinthus amethystinus	occasionally
Iris anglica, I. hispanica and *I. hollandica*	
Ixia hybrids	
Leucojum vernum	occasionally
Lilium — practically all species and garden varieties	
Muscari — all species	
Narcissus — all garden varieties	
Nerine bowdenii	
Tigridia pavonia	
Trillium grandiflorum	
Tulipa — all taller garden varieties	

Bulbs with Special Requirements

Lime in the soil in sufficient quantity is a must for:
  all species of *Cyclamen, Lilium candidum, L. chalcedonicum, L. henryi, L. longiflorum* and *L. martagon.*

Lime in the soil is not tolerated by:
  Lilium auratum, L. dauricum, L. formosanum, L. speciosum, L. tigrinum and the Bellingham Hybrids. Acidic soil is required by all species of *Trillium.*

Damp locations are necessary for:
  Bulbocodium vernum and *Colchicum autumnale* and all species of *Arum* and *Leucojum.*

Semi-shade is required (not just tolerated) by:
  all species of *Arum, Cyclamen, Erythronium, Leucojum* and *Trillium.*

Semi-shade is preferred by:
  all species of *Chionodoxa.* It is also important for most species of *Lilium.*

Full sun is required by:
  all species of *Crocosmia, Eremurus, Eucomis, Gladiolus, Tigridia, Iris reticulata,* and most species of *Allium.*

Of the lilies the following may be planted in full sun:
  Lilium longiflorum, L. pardalinum, L. pumilum, L. regale, L. superbum, L. tigrinum and the Mid Century Hybrids.

Plates

The measurement below the family name denotes the plant's average height and the months refer to the flowering period. The individual plants are arranged, broadly speaking, in the order in which they flower rather than in any botanical order.

Winter Aconite

Ranunculaceae

4 in.

February to March

Eranthis SALISB.

The winter aconite is one of the earliest of all flowers. If the ground is not frozen it often begins to blossom while still covered with a blanket of snow, usually at the end of February. A native of southern Europe, it was described as early as 1570.

The flowering stem is the first thing to appear from the irregularly formed tuber, for the palmate, emarginate leaves do not develop till after the flowering period. Borne on the stem, which is about 4 in. high, is a single, bright yellow blossom, $\frac{3}{4}$ to 1 in. in diameter. Since the petals serve as a nectary (a gland that secretes nectar) it is the sepals that form the conspicuous part of the flower. Below this is a rosette of divided leafy bracts with the flower set in the centre. Most widely cultivated are the species *Eranthis hyemalis*, a native of the western part of southern Europe from France to Bulgaria, and *Eranthis cilicica*, indigenous to Greece and Turkey and differing from the former in having the leafy bracts of the rosette more finely segmented. The flower is a deeper yellow and the leaves are tinted bronze. A hybrid between these two species is *E.* × *tubergenii*, which has larger flowers and a longer flowering period than either of its parents. Sometimes listed in catalogues is the form 'Guinea Gold' with larger flowers and bright green leaves.

Winter aconites are quite hardy, thriving in moist soils rich in humus. The tubers should be planted in early autumn, best of all in September, at a depth of 2 in. Damp locations under trees and shrubs are particularly suitable, also moist spots in the rock garden or nearby. The plant is readily propagated from seed, which should be sown immediately after harvesting, the flowers appearing in the third year. Winter aconites do best in a permanent site, without transplanting, where, if conditions are favourable they will spread freely through self-sown seedlings.

Bulbocodium vernum L.

syn. *Colchicum bulbocodium* KER-GAWL.
  Colchicum vernum (L.) KER-GAWL.

Liliaceae
4 in.
March to April

The less commonly cultivated bulbocodium bears a flower resembling a small colchicum and in the opinion of some botanists should be assigned to the genus *Colchicum*. An early-flowering plant, with the blossoms sometimes appearing before the end of February, it is native to southern Europe, from the Pyrenees to the Caucasus, where it grows at elevations up to 6,500 ft.

The corm is large, about 1 in. across, with brown-black skin. Larger corms produce several flowers. These are borne on a short stem so that the plant is no more than 4 in. high. The narrow, strap-shaped leaves appear after the flowering period and grow to a length of about 10 in. The flowers are violet-pink, about $1\frac{1}{2}$ in. across, the petals long and narrow, without any discernible difference in width from base to tip.

Bulbocodiums do best in a sunny aspect, even though they tolerate semi-shade and moist sandy soil. In the wild they grow on mountain meadows. If planted in poorer soil, topdress with compost in the autumn.

Propagation is by offsets, which in a favourable location form whole clumps of plants. The corms should be planted 3 to 4 in. deep in August to September. Good places to plant are moist lawns or near a rock garden with snowflakes, aconites and certain crocuses as companions.

Bulbocodiums greatly resemble merenderas for which they are sometimes mistaken. Merenderas, however, are not as hardy and are usually grown in alpine houses.

Common Snowdrop
Galanthus nivalis L.

Amaryllidaceae
6 to 8 in.
February to March

Snowdrops are the best known spring flowers, the small bunches sold at the flower stalls being the first herald of nature's awakening from her winter sleep. The most widely cultivated is the species *G. nivalis*, native to southern and central Europe.

The bulb is small and ovoid, about 2 in. in circumference. The long, narrow leaves, up to 6 to 10 in. in length, are grooved down the centre and appear practically at the same time as the flowers. The flower, generally only one on a stalk, is pendulous and borne on a short pedicel which grows from the same point as the spathe, the protective covering of the bud. The three outer segments of the perianth are longer, spoon-shaped, white, and stand away from the inner segments which are shorter with a small notch at the lower end and above the notch a horizontal green band. The outer segments are about $\frac{3}{4}$ in. long, the inner ones half that.

Galanthus nivalis has several varieties: *G. n. flore pleno*, a double form described as long ago as 1731, which has only the inner segments of the perianth doubled; *G. n. atkinsii*, taller, with large green blotches, flowering very early, and *G. n.* 'S.Arnott', pretty, with conspicuous green blotches on the inner segments, 10 in. tall, with a pleasant fragrance.

Snowdrops prefer light soils with plenty of humus and moisture and do quite well in semi-shade.

Propagation is usually by means of offsets which are comparatively large and thus flower the following season. The bulbs should be planted about 2 in. deep in September under trees and shrubs; if they are set out in the rock garden then only in spots with sufficient humus. After a time they form nice clumps and in the wild often seed themselves and spread freely. Snowdrops are also cultivated in bowls.

Snowflake

Leucojum vernum L.

Amaryllidaceae
10 to 12 in.
February to March

Snowflakes are just as popular and have the same distribution as snowdrops, to which they bear a marked resemblance. The difference is mainly in the flower, which is symmetrically bell-shaped with the six segments of the perianth of equal length. The commonest species is *L. vernum*, native to Europe and known since 1420.

The snowflake has a small, ovoid bulb, and dark green, longish, narrow leaves with a shallow groove in the centre. The plant grows to a height of 10 to 12 in. The flowers are usually single and about ¾ in. in diameter. They are a creamy-white with a green to yellow-green spot on each of the six segments. Some varieties have yellower spots or two flowers to a stem.

Snowflakes prefer moist locations and in the wild are often found growing in meadows that are very wet in spring. They like deep soil rich in humus and stand up well to shade. Propagation is by means of seeds or offsets, which should be planted about 4 in. deep in August to September. They should not be stored for any length of time, otherwise the bulbs will dry out. When raised from seed, which may be sown directly in the flower bed, the plants bear flowers in the second year. Snowflakes are planted in the same way as snowdrops, often in combination with the latter, in damp meadows; they will also grow in the shade of trees and shrubs.

Also cultivated in some places is the species *L. aestivum*, which grows in central and eastern Europe and as far as Asia, is more than 20 in. tall, has long, narrow leaves and bears clusters of 3 to 7 flowers on a single stem. The individual flowers are ½ to ¾ in. in diameter and are borne on pedicels of unequal length in April to May. *L. autumnale*, native to Portugal, Spain, Sardinia and Sicily, is 4 to 8 in. tall and the flowers, with small, pale red spots at the base of the segments, and up to 3 on a stem, are borne in August and September. This species requires a warmer situation.

Dwarf Iris
Iris reticulata M.B.

Iridaceae
6 to 8 in.
February to March

The best known of the dwarf, bulbous irises are *I. reticulata*, *I. danfordiae* and *I. histrioides*. *I. reticulata*, native to the Caucasus, is a beautiful, early flowering (February to March) species and the hardiest of the three.

The bulb consists of a single, flattened, fleshy scale with pale reticulate coat. Unlike the rhizomatous irises the growing period ends in summer and the roots die away annually. The stalk is very short and leafless. The plants are 6 to 8 in. tall, but the leaves, which are very small during the flowering period, later grow to a length of 12 in. They are narrow, linear, and angular in cross-section. The flowers are single with a long perianth tube similar to the crocus. The inner petals (standards) are vertical, the outer ones (falls) grow out half-vertically and then droop. The diameter of the flower is about $2\frac{1}{2}$ in.

I. reticulata is a deep blue-mauve but in the wild one may come upon various other shades ranging from reddish-mauve to dark blue. The blade of the fall has a yellow 'tongue' bordered with white spots. Various forms of this species are cultivated in gardens, namely 'Cantab', pale blue, 'Harmony' and 'Joyce', deep sky blue and 'J. S. Dijt', reddish-purple.

These plants should be put in a sheltered site in the sun in light soil with good drainage. They are generally planted in sunny spots in the rock garden but may also be forced in pots or bowls, like crocuses.

Propagation is by means of offsets, produced in ample numbers when conditions are favourable, which take two years to develop. They should be planted 3 in. deep in September.

Crocus chrysanthus HERB.

Iridaceae
2 to 3 in.
February

Crocuses are favourite spring flowers. Most widely distributed are the large-flowered horticultural varieties but the botanical species and their hybrids are becoming increasingly popular. The most important of these is *C. chrysanthus*. It has been known only since 1847 but has given rise to more than 60 registered hybrids to date, this being the speciality of E. A. Bowles of England. The parent species, not cultivated in gardens, is native to Greece and Asia Minor.

The corms are small and round with a smooth, firm, light-coloured tunic. The narrow leaves with white stripes appear, as a rule, together with the flowers. A single corm produces 4 to 10 flowers with a long perianth tube on a markedly abbreviated pedicel. The flowers are globular, the petals broad, with rounded or bluntly pointed tips. The species is yellow but the varieties are white, yellow and blue. The most important white forms are: 'Snow Bunting', 'Warley White' and 'Ladykiller'; yellow forms: 'Advance', 'Cream Beauty', 'E. A. Bowles', 'E. P. Bowles', 'Fuscotinctus', 'Goldilocks', 'Mariette', 'Nanette', 'Saturnus' and 'Zwanenburg Bronze'; blue forms: 'Blue Bird,' 'Blue Pearl', 'Blue Peter' and 'Princess Beatrix'.

Crocuses have no special requirements. However, the soil should be well drained and rich in humus and the situation a sunny one (even though crocuses tolerate partial shade), moist in spring and dry in summer.

The varieties are propagated by cormlets, which most forms produce in abundance. They should be planted 3 in. deep in September and October and may be left undisturbed for several years. Crocuses are usually planted in the rock garden, strong-growing varieties also in grass, but there they lose their vigour after a few years.

Crocus sieberi J. GAY

Iridaceae
1¾ to 2 in.
February to March

Crocus sieberi is likewise a lovely and popular species cultivated in several varieties. It flowers only a few days later than *C. chrysanthus* and is generally somewhat smaller. Its native habitat is Crete and Greece.

The corm is round with a finely reticulated tunic. The narrow leaves appear either together with the flowers or after they have faded. Five to eight flowers are produced by a single corm. They are pinkish-mauve to bluish-mauve, the colour showing marked variation, but in all forms they have an orange-yellow throat.

C. sieberi tricolor is a purplish-blue variety; 'Firefly' has the inner segments pale mauve and the outer ones almost white; in 'Hubert Edelsten', a very striking form, the outer segments are purple with white horizontal bands, the inner segments silvery-mauve; 'Violet Queen' is a small form with delicate mauve flowers. There is also a pure white form, raised by E. A. Bowles and known as 'Bowles's White', which is the whitest of all small spring crocuses.

C. sieberi is a good garden species. It has no special requirements and is usually easy to propagate, best of all by means of the small cormlets so that it will come true to type. It is generally planted in the rock garden.

Crocus biflorus MILL.

Iridaceae
2 to 2½ in.
February to March

Crocus biflorus is another of the cultivated botanical species of crocus, distinguished from the garden forms by its earlier flowering (usually mid-February to March) and smaller size. It grows naturally in the wild in Italy, the Balkans, Asia Minor and Iran.

The corm is globose with a firm tunic, which separates at the base into narrow bands. The leaves, narrow and with a white stripe, generally appear together with the flowers. A larger corm produces several flowers, which, as in all crocuses, have a long perianth tube. The flowers are star-shaped, about 1½ in. across, with bluntly tipped segments. The species is white with purple stripes on the outside. A number of varieties are grown in gardens, namely *C. b. adamicus*, tinted pale mauve, deep mauve outside; *C. b. alexandri*, pure white, deep purple outside; *C. b. argenteus*, a very early white variety; *C. b. parkinsonii*, creamy white, *C. b. weldenii*, white, mauve outside.

Crocus biflorus has modest requirements as regards soil and location and can be grown under the same conditions as *C. chrysanthus*. Certain varieties, such as *C. b. alexandri*, however, are somewhat more tender and in colder areas should be provided with a light cover in winter. It is recommended to place poisoned bait for killing mice under the cover of leaves or fir boughs as these pests often do great damage to crocuses. The cover should be removed early in spring.

Propagation is by cormlets and seeds. This species may be left in the same spot for several years. It is planted chiefly in the rock garden or nearby.

Crocus vernus HILL

Iridaceae
2 to 3½ in.
February to March

The term *Crocus vernus* embraces all the large-flowered garden varieties raised mainly in Holland, which, compared with most of the wild species, are taller and bear flowers later.

The forms of these crocuses are globose or slightly flattened, up to 4¼ in. in circumference, and covered with a pale reticulated tunic. The leaves are generally broader than in the species, slightly narrowed at either end and with a conspicuous white band. Flowering plants are usually no taller than 5 in. but the leaves are longer. The flowers are almost always broadly rounded, as are the individual segments. Recommended varieties include: white, 'Jeanne d'Arc', 'Peter Pan' and 'Kathleen Parlow'; blue to deep purple, 'Early Perfection', 'Flower Record', *C. v. purpureus grandiflorus*, 'Queen of the Blues', 'Remembrance' and 'Vanguard'; blue-white or striped purple, 'Cinderella', 'Pickwick' and 'Striped Beauty'. The only yellow large-flowered crocus is 'Dutch Yellow', known also as 'Large Yellow' or 'Yellow Giant'. This variety flowers early and is very floriferous but sterile, and cannot therefore be cross-bred.

Crocuses do well in a rich soil and a sunny aspect. They may be planted in grass, and in this case, they should be supplemented occasionally with larger corms. (The grass must not be cut until the crocus leaves have died down.) Where conditions are good and the corms multiply readily, they should be lifted and divided after two to three years, otherwise they will become too congested. The various forms are propagated by means of cormlets which should be planted 2½ to 3 in. deep in October. They are generally put out in groups, in beds in front of taller bulbs and in the rock garden. They are good for forcing in pots or bowls.

Anemone, Windflower

Anemone blanda SCHOTT and KOTSCHY

Ranunculaceae
4 to 6 in.
March to April

This is a delightful, early-flowering spring anemone, quite small in size, which makes it a popular plant for the rock garden. It is native to Asia Minor and Greece.

The small tubers are globose, though generally flattened, the leaves trifoliate and lobed. The plant grows to a height of 6 in. at the most and the flower is $1\frac{1}{2}$ to 2 in. across. The colour is usually blue, both pale and dark, but may also be mauve, pink or white. This anemone is generally grown in drifts of mixed colours but varieties of a single colour are sometimes desired, for example: 'Bridesmaid', white; 'Charmer', deep pink; 'Pink Star', pink with creamy-yellow centre; 'White Splendour', white; 'Radar', red with a white centre; *A. b. atrocoerulea,* deep violet blue and *A. b. rosea,* bright pink.

Anemone blanda requires a warm situation and well-drained soil. It thrives in the sun but will tolerate semi-shade.

The best method of propagation is by means of seeds. They should be sown as soon as they are ripe, preferably in pots or pans. The tubers take two years to develop. Some pure-coloured varieties are propagated by division so that they always come true. The tubers should be planted 2 in. deep in the autumn. This anemone is generally planted in the rock garden though it also does quite well in the shade of trees.

Very similar to *A. blanda* is the species *A. apennina*. It differs by being somewhat taller, producing a smaller flower and being very hardy.

Hyacinthella azurea
(FENZL.) CHOUARD

Liliaceae

syn. *Hyacinthus azureus* (FENZL.) BAK.
   Muscari azureum FENZL.

6 to 8 in.

March to April

This is a popular spring bulb very similar to muscari, for which it is often mistaken. In catalogues it is often listed under the synonym *Muscari azureum*. It has the same densely clustered heads of flowers but the individual bells open at the mouth into six spreading tips, whereas in muscari they are flask-shaped and constricted at the mouth into six grooves edged with white. Hyacinthella, moreover, flowers earlier, usually in March. It is native to the mountain areas of Asia Minor and is resolutely hardy.

The bulb is small and round with a grey-brown tunic, the leaves linear, and the flowers borne in a dense upright raceme of thirty or more blooms. The plant grows to a height of 8 in. The colour of the species is azure blue. Also cultivated is the pure white *H. a. alba* and *H. a. amphibolis*, an earlier variety with larger flowers.

Hyacinthella azurea prefers a light soil and will do well in practically any situation — sun, semi-shade and even denser shade.

It is easily propagated by offsets, which are produced in ample numbers, as well as by means of seed; in a suitable location it spreads by seeding itself. The bulbs may be left in the same site for a number of years. They should be planted about 4 in. deep in September.

Hyacinthella azurea is often planted in the rock garden, in beds with other spring bulbs, and is excellent in combination with early yellow daffodils and species tulips or the later flowering *Crocus aureus*. It does fairly well even in grass, which, however, should not be cut too soon so as to allow the bulbs to ripen. It is also often grown for cutting.

Glory of the Snow

Chionodoxa BOISS.

Chionodoxa luciliae is a small bulb rarely more than 6 in. high. The small star-shaped flowers greatly resemble those of the squill (scilla), but are distinguished from the latter by the perianth segments being joined instead of separate at the base. It is native to the mountains of Asia Minor and generally flowers in late March.

The bulb is small, the leaves, usually two, narrowly elongate, the flowers some ¾ in. across, blue with a white centre, borne in a loose raceme of two to six blooms. Two varieties, *C. l. alba* and *C. l. rosea* have white and pink flowers respectively, and 'Pink Giant' has larger clusters of fairly large pink flowers. Of the other species those that are found in cultivation include *C. gigantea* with large pale blue flowers; *C. sardensis*, brilliant blue flowers with small white centre and the smaller *C. tmoli*, blue with larger white centre.

Glory of the Snow thrives in almost any location but does best in light soils with plenty of humus and a sunny position. Propagation is by offsets of the bulbs, and in favourable situations it will spread freely by seed. If grown from seed, flowers are borne in the second year, whereas in the case of offsets they are produced the following season. They should be planted about 3 in. deep in September to October in a sunny or slightly shaded position. They are often grown together with other small bulbs in the rock garden, but only in spots where they will not dry out too much during the growing period. They can also be grown in the border as edging. Chionodoxas may be left undisturbed for a number of years. They are also good for forcing in pots.

Siberian Squill

Scilla sibirica ANDR.

Liliaceae
4 to 8 in.
March to April

This popular and best-known member of the genus, distinguished by its brilliant mauve-blue colour, is native to the Balkans, Caucasus and Asia Minor but not Siberia, as its name implies.

The globose bulbs with thin tunic grow to some 4 in. in circumference. The elongate leaves appear together with the flowers but attain their full length later. The flowers are borne in a loose raceme of three to four flowers on a stem some 6 in. high. They are like wide-open bells, usually blue. Frequently cultivated are the white variety *S. s. alba*, the paler blue *S. s. taurica* and the lovely deep blue 'Spring Beauty', more robust and flowering earlier.

Squills have no special requirements but do better in humus-rich, sandy soils and in sun, even though they tolerate semi-shade. In spring adequate moisture is necessary for their growth, in winter drier conditions.

They are readily propagated by means of offsets which should be planted 2 to 3 in. deep at the end of August and may be left undisturbed for a number of years. When transplanting they should not be left in the open for too long because they have a thin tunic and dry out easily. Offsets produce flowers within a year. Propagation by means of seed is also easy, but in this case flowers are not produced until the second year.

Squills are generally planted in the rock garden, where they soon spread through self-sown seedlings to form thick masses. An excellent and welcome characteristic is that they will grow fairly well in grass. They are also good for forcing in pots or bowls.

Puschkinia scilloides ADAMS.

syn. *Adamsia scilloides* (ADAMS.) WILLD.

Liliaceae
4 to 6 in.
March to April

Named after Count Mussin-Pushkin, the Russian chemist, geologist and plant collector, the puschkinia is native to Asia Minor and the Caucasus.

The bulb is small, globose and white, the leaves broadly linear, about ¾ in. wide, and the plant about 6 in. high. The flowers greatly resemble those of *Scilla tubergeniana*. About ½ to 1 in. across, they are borne in dense racemes of ten to twelve flowers. The type species is little known, the form generally cultivated being *P. scilloides libanotica*, which has pale blue to white flowers with a central blue stripe down the outside of the segments. Also cultivated is the white form *P. s. libanotica alba*.

Puschkinia is quite unpretentious in its requirements. Suitable to its growth is a situation with plenty of humus and moisture in the soil during the spring months but dry in summer.

Propagation is both by offsets and from the seed, the latter producing mature bulbs after one year. Bulbs should be planted 3 in. deep in September and may be left undisturbed for a number of years; they spread freely in a suitable site. They tolerate semi-shade and may therefore be planted under trees and shrubs, often together with other small spring bulbs. They are also used in the rock garden.

European Dog's-tooth Violet

Erythronium dens-canis L.

Liliaceae
6 to 8 in.
March to April

The European Dog's-tooth Violet is the only member of the genus *Erythronium* that is native to Europe, where it grows in open broad-leaved woodlands. It is one of the most beautiful of spring bulbs, which does well and is quite hardy in favourable situations. Often, however, it takes a number of years to become established in a new environment.

The name of this species derives from the shape of the corm, which is long and narrow and resembles the canine tooth of a dog. The leaves are broadly lanceolate, grey-green with brown and purple marbling and very decorative in themselves for several months. The plant is never more than 8 in. high and flowers in late March and April. The flowers, borne singly, are pendant with partly recurved segments. The colour of the type species is purplish-pink.

Several pink and mauve forms are cultivated: 'Lilac Wonder', 'Pink Perfection', 'Purple King', 'Rose Beauty' and also a white form, 'Snowflake'.

Erythroniums like moist, but not water-logged, soil with plenty of humus and a semi-shaded position rather than full sun. Since it takes several years for the plants to become established in a new situation they should be left permanently in one spot. Propagation is by offsets, which should be planted about 3 in. deep in September. Species may also be increased by means of seed, in which case the flowers are produced after five years. Erythroniums should be planted in partly shaded situations under trees and shrubs or in a damp spot in the rock garden.

All other species of this genus are native to North America, for example, *E. americanum*, *E. oregonum*, *E. revolutum* and *E. tuolumnense*. In cold districts these species may need to be provided with a cover for the winter.

Daffodil

Narcissus L.

Amaryllidaceae
16 to 20 in.
April

Garden varieties of narcissus are divided into twelve divisions, according to the type of flower. The first division includes all garden forms with corona longer than the perianth segments and known as trumpet narcissi.

Trumpet narcissi are more robust than the other divisions and flower fairly early. In fact, as a group, apart from the original species, they are the earliest to flower and some varieties are very good for forcing. Most are readily propagated and are quite hardy.

All the varieties are propagated by offsets, which should be planted as early as August so that they root before frosts set in. Daffodils growing in a favourable location need not be lifted regularly, but only after a number of years when they become congested and need to be separated. For purposes of propagation they are generally lifted every second year and stored for a short time in a well-ventilated spot, preferably out of doors with a roof-like shelter. Daffodils are grown in flower beds, in grass, and for cutting; they are also good for forcing.

Recommended varieties include:

'Beersheba', 17 in. high, the flower often more than $4\frac{1}{2}$ in. across, with long, slender trumpet; corona and perianth white.

'Content', about 20 in. high with flowers $4\frac{1}{2}$ in. across; perianth creamy-white, corona pale yellow.

'Preamble', about 18 in. tall, bearing a flower $4\frac{1}{2}$ in. across; perianth white, long, yellow corona.

Narcissus L.

The second division of garden varieties is formed by the large-cupped narcissi, in other words those varieties with corona more than one-third but less than equal to the length of the perianth segments.

This group usually flowers a few days later than the trumpet narcissi and exhibits greater variation in the shape of the corona, which may be like a short trumpet, have a widely or little expanded mouth, be smooth or with frilled edge, open, flat, as well as wavy or frilled on the entire surface. The corona is also more strikingly coloured, in many cases orange to red, salmon to rose pink with only the edge brightly coloured, in other instances brightly coloured throughout.

The methods of propagation and uses are the same as for the trumpet narcissi.

Recommended varieties include:

'Easter Bonnet', 15 in. high, the flowers 3½ in. across, the perianth segments slightly wavy, corona an expanded trumpet with broad, markedly wavy edge. Perianth creamy white, corona pale apricot-orange with salmon-pink edge.

'Polindra', more than 20 in. high, the flowers 4 in. across. Perianth segments smooth, white, corona a widely expanded, bright yellow cup with slightly frilled edge.

Narcissus L.

The illustrated varieties are likewise from the large-cupped group.

'Belisana', beautiful and large, up to 20 in. tall with flowers up to 5 in. across. The perianth segments are broadly oval, deeply overlapping and slightly recurved, the corona expanded and very wavy. Perianth white, corona yellow with broad, bright orange edge.

'Signal Light', 18 in. tall with flowers $4\frac{1}{2}$ in. across. The overlapping, broadly oval perianth segments terminate in a point. The corona is a shallow cup only slightly wavy at the edge. Perianth creamy white, corona pale orange.

'Tannhäuser', 20 in. tall with flowers $3\frac{1}{2}$ in. in diameter. The perianth segments are broadly oval, overlapping, smooth. The corona is fairly flat with a faintly wavy edge. Perianth yellow, corona yellow with orange-red edge.

All the above forms are generally planted in beds or used for forcing. With standard care they grow well and are certain to flower.

Narcissus L.

Amaryllidaceae
16 to 18 in.
April to May

The third division of narcissi includes the small-cupped varieties with the corona not more than one third the length of the perianth segments. The members of this group often have a brightly coloured corona but show less variation in shape. They also flower later than the trumpet narcissi.

The methods of propagation and uses are the same as in the preceding groups.

Recommended varieties include:

'Apricot Distinction', about 17 in. high with flowers $3\frac{1}{2}$ in. across. The broadly oval perianth segments are an unusual colour — pale apricot-pink; the corona, a bright reddish-orange, is flat with finely indented margin.

'Blarney', almost 20 in. high with flowers about 4 in. in diameter. The perianth segments are smooth and pure white, the corona shallow to flat, coloured orange with pale primrose-yellow rim.

'Chungking', 18 in. high with flowers about $3\frac{1}{2}$ in. across. The perianth segments are firm and smooth, broadly oval, overlapping and coloured bright yellow. The corona is shallow, expanded, with a finely indented rim; it is coloured a uniform orange-red.

Narcissus L.

The fourth division of narcissi includes all the double forms, both single and multi-flowered. Either the whole flower may be double, the corona thus being indiscernible, or else only the corona.

These forms, too, may be cultivated in the same way as the trumpet narcissi.

Recommended varieties include:

'Golden Castle', about 18 in. tall with a fairly full flower almost 4 in. in diameter. The outside perianth segments are creamy-white, the inside ones bright yellow.

'Hollandia', about 12 in. high, with flowers $3\frac{1}{2}$ in. across. The nicely shaped double corona is orange, the perianth pale yellow.

Some of these forms are difficult to propagate. Only those that are good for forcing are cultivated widely, for example 'Cheerfulness' and 'Yellow Cheerfulness', 'Irene Copeland', 'Van Sion', sometimes also 'Daphne', 'Indian Chief', 'Texas' and 'Twink'.

Angel's Tears
Narcissus triandrus L.

Amaryllidaceae
6 to 14 in.
April to May

Narcissus triandrus is a very pretty but tender species, native to Spain and Portugal. It occurs in several varieties differing in the size and shape of the flower. All, however, are 6 to 14 in. high and may have several flowers on a stem. The flowers have slightly reflexed perianth segments and a fairly long, cup-shaped corona. The forms vary in colour from white to cream and yellow.

The cross-breeding of *N. triandrus* with other species and varieties gave rise to the fifth division of narcissi — the Triandrus narcissi. All members of this group have the characteristic features of the type and thus bear clear evidence of their origin.

Narcissus triandrus is rather tender and is best grown in sheltered positions. In hard winters some protection may be necessary. The varieties are hardier but again may require protection against frosts. The soil should be a well-drained, fairly rich loam, and the situation a sunny one.

The species may be increased by means of seed, the varieties only by offsets, which should be planted in August.

Recommended varieties include:

'Dawn', about 14 in. high with one to two flowers on a stem. These may be up to $3\frac{1}{4}$ in. across; the corona is flat and both perianth and corona are coloured pale yellow.

'Hawera', 10 in. high and often with four flowers on a stem. The flowers are $1\frac{1}{2}$ in. across at the most, entirely yellow with a short, closed corona.

'Thalia', 14 in. high at the most, usually with three flowers on a stem. The flowers, 3 in. across and creamy-white, have a long corona. This is a beautiful and dainty form.

Narcissus cyclamineus D.C.

Amaryllidaceae
4 to 12 in.
February to March

Narcissus cyclamineus is a lovely small daffodil with small single flowers on stems 6 in. high at the most. The corona is long and smooth with a slightly wavy rim, the perianth segments are recurved, and the colour is a rich yellow. It grows in damper situations in northern Portugal and Spain.

Crosses between *N. cyclamineus* and other species have produced a number of hybrids classed as division six. All members of this group have the basic characteristics of *N. cyclamineus*, namely more or less strongly recurved segments and usually only slightly frilled corona, which may be long or short, depending on the given variety.

N. cyclamineus requires moist soil but with good drainage, likes semi-shade and should be supplied with a protective covering during harsh winters. The garden varieties are hardier and more adaptable.

Varieties are propagated by offsets, the species also by means of seeds. The bulbs should be planted in August and lifted up every few years when they become congested and need to be separated.

Recommended varieties include:

'Jenny', up to 12 in. high with fairly large flower up to $2\frac{3}{4}$ in. in diameter, and the corona long, broad and pale yellow.

'Jumblie', about 8 in. high with flowers 2 in. across, the corona long, slender and bright yellow. This form bears two to three flowers on each stem.

'Peeping Tom', an excellent variety about 12 in. high with flowers up to $3\frac{1}{2}$ in. across. The corona is long and slender, the colour a deep yellow. The flowers are very persistent.

Narcissus jonquilla L.

Amaryllidaceae
8 to 12 in.
April

This species is native to southern Europe, chiefly Spain, but also Dalmatia and North Africa (Algeria).

Narcissus jonquilla grows to a height of 8 to 12 in. and is a multi-flowered plant usually bearing two to six flowers to a stem. The corona is fairly short and the perianth segments broadly oval, about 1 in. across. The colour is yellow and they have a delicate but penetrating scent.

Like *N. cyclamineus*, this species is also often crossed with others and the hybrids which have retained the basic characteristics of the type are classed as a separate group — division seven, further subdivided according to the length of the corona.

Narcissus jonquilla is slightly tender and requires a protective cover in winter in cold areas; the varieties are hardier. It prefers a fairly rich soil with good drainage and a sunny aspect.

Varieties are propagated by offsets which should be planted in August. They should also be lifted up and divided every few years in the month of July. As for the type species, it is not often propagated.

Pictured together with *N. jonquilla* is the variety 'Tittle-Tattle', which is about 16 in. high with two to three flowers on a stem, the individual flowers being about $2\frac{1}{4}$ in. across, the corona a shallow cup; the perianth is pale yellow, the corona a deeper shade.

Narcissus jonquilla may be cultivated only in sheltered locations; the varieties are good for garden decoration, planting in grass and cutting.

Narcissus tazetta L.

Amaryllidaceae
12 to 20 in.
February to March

Narcissus tazetta is a sweet-scented, multiflowered species indigenous to warmer areas and therefore quite tender. There are countless wild forms growing in northern Spain, Portugal, the Mediterranean region, Asia Minor and Iran. Forms growing in China and Japan differ from the others in having larger flowers and are imported into Europe and cultivated under glass, generally as forced blooms for the Christmas season.

The species and its forms are never more than 12 in. high; garden varieties may grow to a height of more than 20 in. *N. tazetta* and its hybrids have up to ten flowers on a stem. The perianth segments are fairly broad and the corona short.

Narcissus tazetta can be grown only in truly warm and sheltered locations, but hybrids raised from crosses with double garden varieties are quite hardy. They are widely grown in the garden and as cut flowers, and some are excellent for forcing. They require the same conditions as other garden narcissi. The soil should be deep and with good drainage and a light covering should be provided in winter.

Recommended varieties include:

'Laurens Koster', a variety that was introduced as early as 1906 but is still one of the best forms. About 16 in. high, it has up to seven flowers on a stem. These are some $1\frac{3}{4}$ in. across. The perianth segments are creamy white, the short corona orange-yellow.

'Scarlet Gem', is likewise an old variety dating from 1910 with four to six flowers on a stem about 16 in. high. The perianth is golden-yellow, the short, wavy corona orange. The flowers measure $1\frac{3}{4}$ in. in diameter. This is an excellent variety for late forcing.

Tulipa violacea BOISS. and BUHSE

Liliaceae
6 in.
March

This is a delicate, pinkish-purple to mauve tulip, one of the first
to flower, usually as early as the beginning of March. It is native
to the mountains of northern Iran, where it was discovered at
elevations of about 12,000 ft.

The bulb is ovoid with firm, yellowish to reddish tunic and
hairs at the apex. This tulip is rarely taller than 6 in. The leaves
form a ground rosette, the flower is cup-shaped, 1½ to 1¾ in. in
diameter, and opens wide in the sun. The colour is pinkish-
purple with a brown-black basal blotch. Also frequently
cultivated is the form *T. v.* 'Yellow Centre', which, as the name
implies, has a yellow basal blotch, is pinkish-mauve and flowers
up to a week later. There is also a white form — *T. v. pallida*
with a small blue-violet basal blotch.

Tulipa violacea is popular with gardeners because it is so
attractive in the rock garden. It should be planted about 4 in.
deep in October in a warm, sunny situation in a good, medium
loam soil. In colder areas a light cover should be provided
during the winter. Propagation is by offsets, which are not as
plentiful as in *T. tarda*, for example, but in favourable conditions
it spreads quite readily to form nice clumps. It may be left undisturbed for a number of years.

Water-lily Tulip

Tulipa kaufmanniana REGEL.

Liliaceae
4 to 10 in.
March to April

Early flowering and easy cultivation make this species, native to Turkestan, one of the most popular and widespread of the botanical tulips.

The bulb is ovoid with a brown, papery tunic. Depending on the variety or form the plant grows to a height of 4 to 10 in. The leaves are grey-green, with brownish-purple markings in some hybrids. The perianth segments are narrow, elliptic, bluntly tipped, opening into a star in the sun. The diameter of the flower may be 2 to 3 in. The colour of the species is creamy-yellow with a large yellow basal blotch, often edged with red spots of varying size and intensity. The perianth segments have silvery or carmine-pink markings on the outside, usually a deeper hue in the varieties. There are a number of hybrids and varieties coloured white, all shades of yellow, orange to scarlet. The most highly valued include 'Alfred Cortot', 'Ancilla', 'Berlioz', 'Brilliant', 'César Franck', 'Corona', 'Fritz Kreisler', 'Heart's Delight', 'Johann Strauss', 'Josef Kafka', 'Scarlet Elegance', 'Shakespeare', 'Solanus', 'Stresa', 'The First' and 'Vivaldi'.

T. kaufmanniana and its hybrids require no special care, though like all other tulip species they do better in deep soil with plenty of humus and in a sunny situation.

The forms and varieties are propagated by offsets, which are produced in fair quantities in most instances. The bulblets should be planted 4 to 6 in. deep in October. Offsets often form on stolons, sometimes at depths of more than 8 in. This tulip is good for planting in the open, the smaller varieties are also suitable for the rock garden. It grows reasonably well when naturalized in grass.

Tulipa fosteriana IRVING

Liliaceae
8 to 16 in.
April

A spectacular tulip with large, bright scarlet, glossy flowers, native to Central Asia around Samarkand and Bokhara. Several varieties are grown, and a great number of hybrids have been produced in the past two decades.

Tulipa fosteriana has a large bulb with a thin, papery tunic coloured purplish-brown to reddish and with hairs on the inside. The leaves are broad, grey-green, occasionally olive green, and sometimes glossy *(T. f.* 'Cantata'*)*. The height is 8 to 16 in. depending on the variety. The perianth segments are elliptic and bluntly pointed at the apex. The colour of the type species and its varieties is a glossy crimson-scarlet. The basal blotch is usually black with a yellow margin, but may sometimes be completely yellow *(T. f.* 'Defiance'*)*. The flower may measure up to 6 in. in diameter.

Tulipa fosteriana is cultivated similarly to other tulips. It has no special requirements, but the soil should be sufficiently rich and the plant well exposed to the sun if it is to flower properly. In damp weather it is sometimes attacked by the disease called fire or tulip mould.

It is a lovely species, best suited for planting in the open, where it flowers earlier than all the garden varieties. Taller hybrids may also be used for cutting, but they do not last long.

The best-known varieties are 'Princeps' and 'Red Emperor'. The loveliest hybrids, whose colours include white, yellow, pink, orange and red are: 'Albas', 'Easter Parade', 'Feu Superbe', 'Pinkeen', 'Purissima' and 'Rockery Beauty'.

Tulipa tarda STAPF.

syn. *Tulipa dasystemon* HORT. NON REGEL.

Liliaceae
4 to 5 in.
April to May

One of the most rewarding of the dwarf species tulips, *T. tarda*, is resolutely hardy, easily propagated and popular as a rock garden plant.

It is native to eastern Turkestan and flowers about two weeks later than *T. kaufmanniana* or *T. violacea*. The bulb is smaller, with a thin yellow tunic. The leaves are narrow, almost prostrate, and form a ground rosette. The stem is short, up to 5 in. at the most, with one to eight flowers borne on short pedicels. The perianth segments are fairly narrow and bluntly tipped at the apex. The small, star-like flowers, $1\frac{1}{2}$ to $1\frac{3}{4}$ in. across, are white. The perianth segments are tinged green to purple outside, yellowish inside.

T. tarda is cultivated in the same way as other tulips. It is readily propagated by offsets which are separated from the bulb when it is lifted. In horticultural establishments it is lifted annually but in gardens it may be left undisturbed for several years. The bulblets should be planted in October, about 4 in. deep. In order to have larger bulbs that produce a greater number of flowers the soil should be rich and loose. The same conditions should be provided in the rock garden. *T. tarda* may also be planted in grass but there it loses its vigour after a time. Nevertheless, it is the best dwarf tulip for this purpose.

Tulipa greigii REGEL.

Tulipa greigii is not usually cultivated in its original form, mainly because it rarely produces offsets and must be propagated by means of seeds. However, there are many hybrids which are extremely attractive. The most striking characteristic of this species is the leaves with their prominent markings which are very decorative in themselves even before the flowers appear. *T. greigii* is native to Turkestan. The species is late-flowering, generally not until May, but the hybrids flower earlier.

The bulb is ovoid with a brown papery tunic. The markings on the leaves in the species are usually in the form of interrupted longitudinal, brownish-purple stripes; in the hybrids the stripes are continuous and the colour varies in intensity. The plant is 8 to 12 in. high, the flower 3 to 5 in. across. The perianth segments are broader at the base and fairly broad towards the apex; the outside ones are reflexed, the inside segments more erect. All, however, are slightly pointed at the apex. The ground colour is orange-red; the basal blotch is olive green, broadly margined with yellow. Many beautiful hybrids coloured various shades of yellow, orange, scarlet, pink and salmon pink have been produced in the past several decades. The most important ones are: 'Cape Cod', 'Jessica', 'Margaret Herbst', 'Oratorio', 'Oriental Splendour', 'Pandour', 'Perlina', 'Plaisir', 'Red Riding Hood', 'Yellow Dawn' and 'Zampa'.

Like all other tall tulips *T. greigii* requires deep nourishing soil with good drainage and a sunny aspect.

All cultivated forms and varieties are propagated fairly easily by means of offsets. These should be planted 6 in. deep in October (small bulblets at a shallower depth), generally in masses in the open. *T. greigii* flowers at about the same time as garden varieties, but the leaves, with their attractive markings, make it a decorative element for a far longer time.

The Lady Tulip
Tulipa clusiana REDOUTÉ

Liliaceae
10 to 12 in.
April to May

The loveliest of the species tulips grown as garden plants, the
Lady Tulip was already known to the botanist Clusius who
acquired it from Persia as early as 1607. It flowers later than
most other dwarf tulips, practically at the same time as the
garden tulips — generally at the beginning of May. It is native
to the mountains of Iran, Iraq, and Afghanistan.

The bulb is globose, attaining a circumference of $2\frac{1}{2}$ in., with
a brown leathery tunic and a few hairs at the base. The leaves
are narrow with two basal leaves and two smaller stem leaves.
Reaching 10 to 12 in. in height, this tulip has a markedly upright
growth. The flowers, star-like when open and measuring $1\frac{1}{2}$ to
$1\frac{3}{4}$ in. in diameter, are always borne singly. They are pure white,
crimson margined with white outside and with a small purplish
basal blotch. Also cultivated is the variety *T. clusiana* 'Cynthia',
differing from the species in having a pale yellow instead of
white ground.

T. clusiana requires a sheltered, warm, dry situation and deep
soil with good drainage. It should be planted 4 in. deep. It is
not readily propagated by offsets and produces no seed whatso-
ever. *T. clusiana* is a very lovely but somewhat tender species that
requires greater care and attention if it is to hold its own and
multiply. It is usually planted only in small numbers in well-
prepared beds or a suitable spot in the rock garden, where it
should be provided with a light cover for the winter.

Resembling *T. clusiana* is the species *T. stellata* and its
varieties; it is of the same height and colour — white, pinkish
crimson outside, with yellow basal blotch. It grows wild in
Afghanistan and northwest India, also in mountainous areas
at elevations above 11,500 ft. It appears to be somewhat
hardier.

Tulipa hageri HELDR.

Liliaceae
8 in.
April to May

Tulipa hageri, a species found growing wild in Greece and Turkey, is interesting for its unusual orange-brown colour. It flowers later than most species tulips grown in the garden, sometimes not until the beginning of May, but its vigorous and balanced growth make it a pleasant sight.

The bulb is ovoid with a firm brown tunic. The grooved leaves are fairly long and narrow, and dark green in colour edged with red. This tulip is about 8 in. high, the leaves generally longer than the stem. When open the flower is a broadly expanded cup about 2 in. in diameter. The colour is a soft orange-brown, greenish on the outside segments, bronze to brownish red inside. *T. hageri* generally bears only a single flower with a black basal blotch edged with yellow. Also frequently cultivated is the variety *T. hageri splendens*, with up to four flowers on fairly long pedicels on a single, very short stem. The basal blotch in this form is of irregular outline, brown with yellow border.

Tulipa hageri requires well-drained soil and a warm, sunny situation; however, it need not be provided with a cover in winter. Propagation is usually only by offsets. It is generally planted in the rock garden 4 to 5 in. deep in October, the same as other tulips. The best combination is together with tulips of the same group, for example *T. orphanidea* or *T. whittallii*.

Tulipa L.

Double early tulips are highly prized as excellent forms for forcing in bowls. They flower several days later than the single early tulips and all have short stems. Since the bulbs produce fewer offsets than those in other groups of tulips, they are more expensive to buy.

All garden tulips are propagated by means of offsets, which are planted in October. Plant the bulbs at a depth of about 4 in., that is with 4 in. of soil above the tip of the bulb. If the tulips are to flower satisfactorily from one year to the next, the bulbs should be lifted in July, stored for the summer in a dry room or shed and only firm, large bulbs put out in October. Smaller ones may either be discarded or else planted in a separate bed for purposes of propagation.

Although double early tulips are used mostly for forcing, many varieties are also excellent for garden decoration. As a rule, they are not used for cutting.

Like most other double tulips the illustrated variety 'Red Blossom' derives from the old variety 'Murillo'. It is about 11 in. tall and the flower measures at least 4 in. across. It is deep carmine-red outside and deep red inside.

Tulipa L.

Liliaceae
22 to 30 in.
April to May

The group of Darwin hybrids was established in 1952 by D. W. Lefeber of Holland by crossing Darwin tulips with *T. fosteriana*. The resulting varieties caused a sensation with their tall and strong stems and large, beautifully coloured flowers. The first hybrids were mostly a glowing red, later ones were yellow or yellow tinged with red and pink. The first and best known form is 'Apeldoorn', currently the most widely cultivated variety in Holland, used in vast numbers for forcing.

The hybrids generally flower early, only a few days after the single early tulips. They are best suited for planting in the open but may also be used for cutting in view of their long, firm stems; however, they do not last as long in the vase as other garden varieties. Cultivation is the same as for other tulips and all Darwin hybrids are readily propagated.

The illustrated variety 'Gudoshnik' is about 24 in. tall and has a large, broad, oval flower. The ground colour is pale yellow patterned with a dense network of fine red veins.

Tulipa L.

Liliaceae
20 to 26 in.
May

The Darwin tulip group comprises the greatest number of cultivated varieties. It was established in about 1900 thanks to the efforts of the Dutch breeder Krelage. The members of this group are distinguished by strong and tall stems and firm flowers that have a characteristic rectangular shape in cross section. They are generally of a single colour, two-coloured forms being practically nonexistent. Most of the varieties are readily propagated.

Darwin tulips are excellent for outdoor planting. Some varieties are used for late forcing and as cut flowers they are the longest lasting of all tulips.

Recommended varieties include:

'Abe Lenstra', about 24 in. high with a fairly large and firm flower coloured a soft pink outside with delicate pink margin and inside.

'Queen of Bartigons', 27 in. tall with a large delicate pink flower.

'Queen of Night', the best variety of the black tulips, 25 in. tall with a firm flower. The colour is deep chestnut purple, inside almost black-purple.

122

Tulipa L.

The group of lily-flowered tulips includes all varieties with long, usually narrow, pointed petals reflexing as they open to resemble the classic lily shape. These tulips are excellent for cutting, good for bedding, and some are suitable for late forcing, especially 'Aladdin' and 'China Pink', and for February forcing, 'Mariette' and 'Red Shine'. They are fairly easy to propagate — by the same method as other tulips.

Recommended varieties include:

'Burgundy', 24 in. tall with large flowers and sharply pointed petals more than 4 in. long. The stem, however, could well be stronger in view of the flower's size. The colour is a deep mauve.

'West Point', about 22 in. tall with a strong stem and large, nicely shaped flower, likewise with long pointed petals. The flower measures up to 5 in. across when open. The colour is yellow.

Tulipa L.

Liliaceae
16 to 28 in.
May

The group of single, late-flowering tulips, also called cottage tulips, defies a precise description of specific characteristics. It is more of a mixture of all single, late tulips that do not fit into any other division and are therefore widely varied in the shape of the flower, colour and size.

It includes varieties with long, narrow flowers such as 'Halcro', 'Renown', 'Rosy Wings' and 'Smiling Queen', all multiflowered garden varieties and viridiflora tulips, best of which is 'Artist'. During the latest classification of tulips most of those previously classed as breeder tulips were added to this group, for example, 'Dillenburg'. However, in all instances these are late-flowering tulips which cannot be used for forcing and are best for outdoor planting and cutting.

'Temple of Beauty' is a beautiful form bred in 1959. It is strong, up to 30 in. tall, the leaves are patterned with faint brown interrupted stripes and the large flower has pointed, reflexed petals about 5 in. long. The colour is an unusual pinkish orange, carmine outside.

Tulipa L.

Fringed tulips are not only interesting because of the finely fringed edge to the petals but also because of the nicely shaped flower. The several varieties do not belong to a single separate group but are included among the Darwin or the cottage tulips, depending on their origin and shape of flower. Most of them flower very late and are not used for forcing. They are eminently suitable for cutting, make nice arrangements and last a long time. For many years there was only the one form, 'Sundew', coloured a deep red; the others were raised only in the past two decades.

'Swan Wings' is pure white, more than 20 in. tall, with oblong flower and slightly open, finely fringed edge. It belongs to the Darwin group.

'Burns', included in the cottage group, is about 20 in. tall, the flower is somewhat more elongate with markedly reflexed, densely fringed petal margins. The colour is pink.

'Blue Heron', a new variety classed among the Darwin tulips, is almost 20 in. tall with a fairly broad flower and reflexed, densely fringed petal margins. The colour is mauve, the fringed margin a paler mauve.

Tulipa L.

The parrot tulips are distinguished by the shape of the flower with irregular petals, the margin toothed or laciniate, sometimes with unusual outgrowths. The flower is very large. Parrot tulips have never been produced by crossing as yet; all have developed spontaneously as mutations of certain varieties.

They are popular garden plants for their exotic appearance, are suitable for bedding and last fairly well when cut. They are not good for forcing as most are very late-flowering forms. Some old varieties tend to have too weak a stem for the heavy flower so that they are easily bent by wind and rain. Cultivation is the same as with other garden tulips.

'Fantasy' is the offspring of the Darwin tulip 'Clara Butt'. It is 22 in. tall, has a fairly firm flower about $4\frac{3}{4}$ in. across and a strong stem. The colour is salmon-pink with irregular green or brown spots outside. This tulip is still one of the best even though it has been known since 1910.

Of the other parrot tulips the most valuable are: 'Black Parrot', 'Blue Parrot', 'Doorman', 'Orange Favourite', 'Red Champion' and 'Texas Gold'.

Common Hyacinth

Hyacinthus orientalis L.

Liliaceae
8 to 10 in.
April

Hyacinthus was introduced to Vienna from Constantinople in the mid-sixteenth century and thence spread to other gardens throughout Europe. In Holland, which became its second native land, it has been cultivated since the beginning of the seventeenth century. At one time as many as 1800 varieties were grown, and, as in the case of tulips, they were the subject of much speculation in the years 1720—1736, though the hyacinth fever never attained the proportions of the tulipomania. The present assortment is limited to the most valuable market varieties. *H. orientalis* is native to the eastern Mediterranean countries, but today's cultured varieties exhibit practically no resemblance to the species. Their flowers are large, compact clusters with a strong, penetrating fragrance. The varieties are white, yellow, pink, carmine, pale and dark blue and mauve.

Hyacinths require deep, fertile soil rich in humus and a sunny location. Bulbs should be planted about 5 in. deep in October. They are usually lifted every year for they are not provided with sufficient nutrients in a permanent site.

Hyacinths very rarely multiply by themselves; they do not produce offsets and the lengthy process of propagation by means of seeds is carried out only for breeding purposes. The method of propagation by artificial means is described in the chapter on propagation.

Hyacinths are popular plants for forcing in pots and bowls. They are also planted in garden beds, often together with other bulbs.

Hyacinthus orientalis L.

Liliaceae
8 to 10 in.
April

Double hyacinths have been known since the first half of the seventeenth century, but it was not until the first half of the eighteenth century that the Dutch gave them their full attention and were able to offer more than 300 double varieties. By the beginning of the nineteenth century, they had reached the peak of their popularity. At that time their colours ran practically the entire gamut. Nowadays, however, only a few varieties are cultivated, mainly for specialist gardeners. Double hyacinths are generally not suited for early forcing, and since this is one of the most important characteristics of hyacinths, their popularity has waned. Even when grown out of doors they generally flower later than the single types. They are also very full and compact and in most cases that is not in line with the present ideal of cultivated flowers, when greater value is being increasingly placed on the beauty of simplicity.

Of the double varieties those that are most widely cultivated are: 'Chestnut Flower', 'General Köhler', 'Hollyhock', 'Madame Haubensak', 'Madame Sophie' and 'Victory Day'. The illustrated 'Dreadnought' was raised in 1900 from 'Grand Maître'.

The method of cultivation and propagation is the same as with single hyacinths; likewise the various uses.

Crown Imperial
Fritillaria imperialis L.

Liliaceae
3 to 4 ft.
April

This well-known spring bulb is a handsome species distinguished by its height and arrangement of the flowers, one that was a favourite in the gardens of old. It is native to the western Himalayas and flowers, as a rule, in April.

The large yellowish bulb has an unpleasant smell and attains a circumference of more than 8 in. All parts of the plant contain the poisonous alkaloid imperialin. The strong stem is up to 4 ft. high, with numerous long leaves ending in a whorl of leaves and an umbel of pendant bell-like flowers, about $2\frac{1}{2}$ in. across and numbering up to twelve. The flowers are yellow, orange or reddish-brown, depending on the variety. Inside, at the base of the perianth segments, are prominent nectaries which attract insects.

Cultivated varieties include: *F. i. lutea* — yellow flowers, *F. i. lutea maxima* — yellow, larger flowers, *F. i. rubra maxima* — vigorous, with red flowers, 'Aurora' — orange-red and 'Orange Brilliant' — tall and orange brown.

Fritillaries do well in rich, deep soil. They may be left undisturbed for a number of years but must be provided with ample fertilizer. They require a sunny situation even though they tolerate temporary shade. The bulbs should be planted in early autumn, large ones about 8 in. deep. When transplanting, they should be stored in frames with peat for they have a thin tunic and dry out easily. Propagation is by offsets and seed; in the latter case they take three to four years to develop.

Fritillaries are used in group plantings with other perennials and alone in front of shrubs and the like. They die back early.

Snake's Head, Guinea Flower

Fritillaria meleagris L.

Liliaceae
8 to 16 in.
April to May

This is a beautiful and interesting plant, not grown in the garden as often as it deserves. Native to western, central and eastern Europe as far as the Caucasus, it is found in the wild in damp meadows, though in far fewer numbers now than before. It generally flowers in April.

The bulb is small and round, sometimes slightly flattened, and covered with a pale tunic. Both the bulb and plant have an unpleasant smell. The leaves are narrow, linear up the stem, and coloured grey-green. The height is 8 to 16 in.

The flowers are broad bells, one to two on a stem, about $1\frac{1}{2}$ in. long and 1 in. across. The species is carmine to purple, chequered a paler colour to whitish. Cultivated varieties are also white, greenish and varying shades of purple to mauve, some very prominently chequered, others less so. Frequently cultivated forms are: 'Artemis', 'Emperor', 'Orion', 'Pomona' and the white form *F. m. alba*.

Fritillaria meleagris requires a moist location, as its distribution in the wild indicates. It does better in the sun.

Propagation is by offsets, this being the only possible method for varieties. The species, however, is readily propagated by seed, in which case the flowers are not produced until after three years. The bulbs should be planted $2\frac{1}{2}$ to 3 in. deep in early autumn and, as with other fritillaries, must be stored in peat when lifted. They are generally planted on the banks of streams, beside expanses of water and in moist situations in grass.

Star of Bethlehem

Liliaceae

Ornithogalum umbellatum L.

4 to 12 in.

April to May

The Star of Bethlehem is not a striking plant but its attraction lies in the pretty white star-like flowers which look well in the wild garden.

Ornithogalum umbellatum grows wild throughout most of Europe as well as in Asia Minor and northern Africa. It has been known since 1500.

The bulb is ovoid and white, the leaves long and narrow, almost as long as the stem which measures 4 to 12 in. The star-like flowers, their number depending on the size of the bulb, are borne in a large corymb. They are white with a green median stripe down the outside of the segment and usually appear in May. They open late in the morning and close again early, towards evening.

Ornithogalum umbellatum does well in almost any situation, but humus-rich soil that is not too heavy is best. It tolerates sun but thrives in semi-shade. It is easily propagated by means of offsets, which are produced in great numbers. They should be planted about 4 in. deep in early autumn. When transferring them to another site they should be lifted in August. Small bulbs take a year to develop. They may be left undisturbed for a number of years.

Star of Bethlehem should be planted in the rock garden together with other bulbous plants or in lightly wooded areas.

Grape Hyacinth
Muscari MILL.

Liliaceae
3 to 18 in.
March to June

Muscari are popular bulbs often planted in the garden. There are about fifty species native to southern Europe and as far as Asia Minor. They flower from March to June, depending on the species, and are 3 to 18 in. tall.

The one most frequently cultivated is *M. armeniacum*, also called 'Early Giant', which is native to north-eastern Asia Minor and flowers in early May. It has a yellow-white, globose bulb, six to eight narrow leaves forming a ground rosette and a stalk about 8 in. high. The bulb produces several flowers. These are flask-like, narrowed both at the base and mouth, and edged with six white-rimmed teeth. The flowers are borne in a long, dense raceme. The commonest colour is cobalt blue though some varieties are pale or dark blue and in some species also white or pinkish.

Muscari grow in practically any situation, producnig a wealth of flowers if planted in loose, rich soil. They require a greater amount of moisture in spring and do well both in the sun and semi-shade, some even in denser shade.

They are readily propagated by offsets, which they produce in great numbers. If it is not necessary that they should come true to type they are also easily multiplied from seed. The bulblets should be planted 4 to 5 in. deep in early autumn for the ground leaves form a rosette before winter sets in. They may be left undisturbed for a number of years. Muscari are attractive planted together with other bulbs and perennials, under trees, in grass and in front of shrubs; some are also good for cutting and forcing.

Of the other species, those most often cultivated are *M. botryoides*, *M. racemosum*, *M. tubergenianum*, and of the taller ones chiefly *M. comosum*.

Hyacinthus amethystinus L.

syn. *Brimeura amethystina* (L.) SALISB.

Liliaceae
8 to 10 in.
April to May

A less widely cultivated bulb, *Hyacinthus amethystinus* grows wild in the alpine meadows of northern Spain. It is very like *Scilla hispanica* in that it, too, has loose racemes of bell-like flowers but unlike the scilla the perianth segments are long and joined in a tube for part of their length instead of being separate, and they are also smaller.

The bulb is oval with a thin, white tunic, the leaves are narrow-linear, and the height of the stem is 8 to 10 in. The flowers are an attractive porcelain-blue; a white form is also sometimes cultivated.

Hyacinthus amethystinus does well in practically any garden soil though it does better in light, well-drained soil; it also likes sun. It is propagated with comparative ease by offsets as well as by means of seeds; the former should be planted 3 to 4 in. deep in September.

This bulb is valued chiefly for the fact that it flowers after most other small spring bulbs have shed their blooms. It is best planted in a wild section of the garden or at the edge of grass where it will not be cut prematurely, also in the rock garden with other smaller bulbs and as an edging plant in beds of perennials.

Spanish Bluebell

Endymion hispanicus (MILL.) CHOUARD
syn. *Scilla hispanica* MILL.
    Scilla campanulata AIT.

Liliaceae
12 in.
May

The Spanish bluebell, *Endymion hispanicus*, was formerly classified as a scilla, and may still be referred to under this name in some books. Native to Spain and Portugal, it has been known since 1601.

The bulb is quite large, irregularly round, without a tunic and light in colour. The leaves are elongated, narrow, pointed, glossy, and appear late, but before the flowering period. The stem is up to 12 in. high. The flowers — drooping bells about ¾ in. long — are borne in loose racemes of ten to fifteen blooms, generally towards the end of May. The species is violet-blue, but also cultivated are varieties that are varying shades of blue, pink and white. Best known are: 'Blue Queen', 'Excelsior', 'La Grandesse', 'Queen of the Pinks', 'Rose Queen' and 'Skyblue'.

Endymion hispanicus is a vigorous plant that does well in almost any situation. Good results are obtained in medium-heavy, nourishing soil rich in humus and it grows better in the sun and semi-shade.

Propagation is mostly by offsets, particularly if the new plant is to come true to type. Seeds, however, are produced in ample quantity and in the wild the Spanish bluebell often spreads freely to form lovely masses. The bulbs should be lifted and divided every few years whenever they become too congested.

Ideal locations are in clearings near woodland groves, but they may also be planted in beds of perennials and may occasionally be used also for cutting.

Scilla amethystina VIS

Liliaceae
10 to 12 in.
May to June

This is a small bulbous plant bearing a great wealth of small, clear blue flowers in late spring. It is close to *Scilla pratensis* and is considered by some botanists to be a variety of that species. *S. amethystina* is distinguished from *S. pratensis* only by its height, size of the flower, which is larger, and colour of the flower, which is a deeper lilac in *S. pratensis*. *S. amethystina* was introduced by members of the Dutch company Van Tubergen from Dalmatia.

The bulb is ovoid and has a very thin, pale tunic. The plant is 10 to 12 in. high, the leaves are long and narrow, and the small, bell-like flowers are borne in a dense, upright raceme of up to thirty blooms. They are pleasantly scented.

Scilla amethystina will grow in any garden location but does better in a sunny aspect.

Propagation is by offsets and seeds; it also often spreads freely by self-sown seedlings. As in all other scillas the bulbs should not be stored for long because they have a thin tunic and soon dry out. They should be planted 4 to 5 in. deep in September and may be left undisturbed for a number of years.

Not a very conspicuous species, it is planted mostly in wild sections of the garden in the sun, sometimes also in the rock garden and as an edging plant in beds of perennials.

Anemone coronaria L.
De Caen

Ranunculaceae
8 to 16 in.
April to June

Anemone coronaria is a large-flowered, strikingly coloured anemone grown chiefly for cutting. It is native to the Mediterranean countries and is most popular in southern France, especially on the Riviera. Planted in a permanent site it flowers in May.

The black, hard, irregular tuber grows to a circumference of as much as 3 in., the leaves are deeply palmately notched as in parsley, the height varies between 8 and 16 in. and the flower measures 2 to 3 in. across. The colour may be red, blue, pink, mauve or white. Two forms are cultivated: De Caen, a single form, and St. Brigid, semi-double. This anemone is generally sold in a combination of mixed colours but there are also several varieties available in single colours.

The tubers of *A. coronaria* may be dried and stored for varying lengths of time, thus determining the period of flowering. They should be planted in April for flowering in May to June, in June for September flowering and in September to October for early spring flowering. Before planting they should be immersed in tepid water for about a day and then planted 2 to 3 in. deep in the sun, though they also tolerate semi-shade. They do best in rich garden soil, not too dry; in sandy soils they do better with an addition of peat. They require a sheltered site and when planted in autumn a cover of fir boughs. Propagation is either by offsets of the tubers or, for a mixture of colours, by seed which is sown in winter. The plants attain their full size in the second year.

Anemone coronaria is valuable for cutting and may be used to brighten a bed of perennials if the given location is a warm and sheltered one.

Anemonie coronaria L.

St. Brigid

Ranunculaceae
8 to 16 in.
April to June

Anemone coronaria St. Brigid differs from De Caen only in the flowers which are semi-double, as opposed to single, with perianth segments generally in three rows. Fully double forms were also cultivated previously, but these are now practically nonexistent. St. Brigid anemones have the same colours as the De Caen strain and are also grown mostly as mixed colours, though there exist forms such as 'Lord Lieutenant' — dark blue, 'The Admiral' — violet-mauve and 'The Governor' — red.

The plant's requirements, cultivation and uses are the same as in *A. c.* De Caen. Also true of both is that propagation from the seed, which has very good powers of germination, produces a mixture of colours as well as varying types of flowers. Only the varieties are propagated by division of the small tubers.

A. coronaria is excellent for cutting; not only are the colours gay and bright but the flowers last for a long time in the vase. One of the most attractive features from the grower's viewpoint is their ease and reliability of forcing in winter. Forced anemones are also used for cutting.

Wake Robin

Trillium grandiflorum (MICHX.) SALISB.

Liliaceae
8 to 18 in.
May to June

Trillium is an interesting plant which derives its name from the Latin word trilix, meaning triple. This is particularly appropriate since its parts are arranged in threes — a whorl of three inner segments or petals and three outer segments or sepals. Cultivated species of the genus *Trillium* are native to North America, those found in Japan and the Himalayas have not become adapted to cultivation.

The root consists of a thick, short tuberous rhizome and the leaves are oval and pointed. The height shows marked variation and ranges from 8 to 18. in. The flowers are borne singly on a stout pedicel. The three sepals are green, the three petals are white, larger than the sepals, oval, bluntly pointed, erect, or more often broadly expanded. Widely cultivated is the form *T. g. roseum*, interesting for its unusual pink colour. There also exist purple to brownish forms. The flowering period is usually in early May.

Trillium requires a damp location and acid soil, best of all peat, and semi-shade. It is a slow grower but quite hardy. It may remain undisturbed for many years; in fact, frequent transplanting is not at all propitious to its growth.

Propagation is by division of the tuberous rhizomes which are separated at the end of August to the beginning of September and planted about 4 in. deep.

Best locations are semi-shaded spots under trees and shrubs, together with flowers and woodland plants, which require acid soil, often close to expanses of water. Trillium is also good for forcing and sometimes used for cutting.

Camass

Camassia LINDL.

Liliaceae
16 to 36 in.
May to June

Camassia is a late spring bulb distinguished by its loose racemes of delicate star-like flowers. It is not often seen in gardens, though it is quite easy to grow. Native to North America, the following three species are the ones generally cultivated: *C. cusickii* — pale blue, *C. leichtlinii* — tall, creamy white, and *C. quamash*, (sometimes listed as *C. esculenta*) — the smallest of the lot, coloured dark mauve-blue.

The bulb is oval and white; the leaves, long and about 2 in. wide, form a ground rosette. The illustrated *C. cusickii* is 2 to 3 ft. tall with a raceme of as many as a hundred tiny flowers, the petals narrow, opening successively from the bottom up.

This species grows wild in meadows and prairies which are damp in spring and dry in summer. In gardens it is best planted in a moist soil, preferably a heavy loam, and is quite happy with winter dampness. It likes a sunny position, but will tolerate semi-shade.

Propagation is by offsets of the bulb and by seed. The bulbs should be planted about 4 in. deep in September so that they have plenty of time to root. They may be left undisturbed for a number of years.

Camassia is attractive planted in masses in grass as well as in beds of perennials and may also be used for cutting.

156

Arum L.

Araceae
8 to 10 in.
May to June

Arum, a tuberous perennial native to southern Europe, is not a species that is widely cultivated, probably because of its specific requirements. The flowering period is short but the decorative leaves last for quite some time and some species have attractive red berries after the flowers have died.

The leaves are hastate on long stalks, green, often white or mottled brown. The flowers, without the usual petals or sepals, are of two kinds — male and female — borne separately and grouped together in a club-shaped inflorescence called a spadix, shielded by a curved sheath called a spathe. The male flowers are always the uppermost, the female flowers at the bottom with sterile flowers separating them. The flowers are followed by fleshy berries generally coloured red.

Most frequently cultivated is *A. italicum* with a whitish spathe, which generally flowers in May.

The illustrated *A. nigrum* is grown less frequently because it is more tender. It, too, is native to southern Europe. The height is about 10 in. The spathe is green in the lower part and dark purplish in the upper part.

Arum requires damp, humus-rich soil and shade. Propagation is by division of the tubers, or by means of seed, which should be sown as soon as ripe, for it soon loses its power of germination. When grown from seed, flowers are produced within two years.

Suitable locations are shaded, moist sites together with ferns and other damp-loving plants.

Allium karataviense REGEL.

Liliaceae
6 to 8 in.
May

The genus *Allium*, which includes the onion, leek and garlic, embraces some three hundred species many of which are good for garden decoration. The individual species show marked variation, some being small and excellent for the rock garden, others more than 3 ft. tall. They have been enjoying increased popularity lately. *A. karataviense*, native to Turkestan, is a small plant and one of the best known for years. It generally flowers in May though sometimes not till the beginning of June.

The bulb is round and white, the leaves broad, strap-shaped, tinted metallic blue, and lying flat, usually in pairs. The stem, 6 to 8 in. high, is topped by flowers borne in a large, dense, uniformly round white or pinkish umbel. The leaves and inflorescence are a decorative feature in the garden long after the flowers have faded.

Allium karataviense will grow in almost any situation though it does better in light, well-drained soil like most members of the onion family. It tolerates dry conditions fairly well and is frost-hardy. Unlike most other species, it tolerates semi-shade.

Propagation is by offsets from the bulb or by seeds; in a suitable site it will spread freely by self-sown seedlings. It takes three years for it to develop from the seed. Bulbs should be planted about 4 in. deep in September to early November. They should be left undisturbed for a number of years for they do not develop fully till the second or third year.

Allium karataviense is suitable for a sunny as well as semi-shaded bed and also for the large rock garden.

Allium moly L.
Allium ostrowskianum REGEL.
syn. *Allium oreophilum ostrowskianum*

Liliaceae
8 to 12 in.
June to July

Allium moly and *A. ostrowskianum* are lovely species that are excellent for the rock garden in a sunny, dry spot.

Allium moly is native to southern Europe, growing mainly in the Pyrenees. It flowers in June and July. The bulb is white, fairly small, round, the leaves grey-green, lanceolate, upright. The small, golden-yellow, star-like flowers are borne in many-flowered, flat umbels on round stems 8 to 12 in. high. A robust plant may have as many as forty flowers.

Allium ostrowskianum is native to Turkestan and flowers at about the same time as *A. moly*. The bulb is round, yellow-white, the leaves narrow, grey-green, prostrate. The plant is about 12 in. high or less, with large, round umbels of fairly large, dark pink to purplish-red flowers.

Both species do well in practically any situation. *A. moly* is resolutely hardy and even *A. ostrowskianum* does not require a cover during the winter even though it needs a warmer, sunny position. *A. moly* also tolerates semi-shade.

Propagation in both instances is by offsets from the bulb and by seed. *A. moly* often spreads freely by self-sown seed. Bulbs of both species should be planted in the autumn about 3 to 4 in. deep in sunny beds and in the rock garden; *A. moly* also in semi-shaded locations.

Allium pulchellum G. DON.

Liliaceae
12 to 20 in.
July to August

This pretty wild garlic, flowering in midsummer, is native to the Mediterranean region. The bulbs have scales with black markings, the leaves are linear with rough edges, and the stem is 12 to 20 in. high.

The small flowers in large umbels have pedicels of unequal length so that the inflorescence looks very light and airy. Interesting are the long, pendant buds. The individual flowers have oval petals and long stamens projecting beyond them. The colour is violet-pink with a darker median stripe on the segments. Often available is the very pretty and hardy white variety.

Allium pulchellum will grow in almost any soil and is a hardy plant but requires a sunny aspect. It is suitable for bedding and is often used for cutting.

Propagation is by offsets from the bulb and by seed, and plants should be left undisturbed in the ground for several years.

Alliums are often unappreciated as ornamental plants, perhaps because of qualms as regards their onion scent, which, however, is not excessively pungent in most instances. Many deserve more widespread cultivation, for they are rewarding and as a rule hardy bulbous plants which are well suited to the modern garden.

Dutch Iris
Iris × hollandica TUV.

Iridaceae
12 to 20 in.
May to June

Iris × hollandica is the horticultural term for varieties raised from the crossing of *Iris xiphium praecox* and *I. tingitana*. According to Rodionienko's new botanical classification these new species belong to a separate genus — *Xiphium*, as do the varieties *Iris × anglica* and *Iris × hispanica*. The type plants of this genus are native to the Pyrenees, southern Italy and northern Africa. Members of the genus *Xiphium* have bulbs made up of three to five fleshy scales, narrow, arched leaves and two to three flowers appearing in succession. They resemble those of *Iris reticulata*.

Iris hollandica, or Dutch Iris, is grown in many varieties which are highly valued for forcing for the cut-flower market. Thermal treatment of the bulbs makes these flowers available in shops for the greater part of the year. The varieties are mostly white, yellow and various shades of blue.

They are very hardy garden plants requiring light, well-drained soil, and an open, sunny position. They can be left in the same position for a few years until they become overcrowded, when they should be lifted. Do this after the foliage has died down, and allow the bulbs a week or two to dry off in an airy shed. Then clean and divide the bulbs, and replant.

Propagation is by offsets which are produced in ample numbers and take two years at the most to develop. They should be planted in early autumn, 3 to 4 in. deep.

These irises are suitable for bedding and excellent for cutting. Most highly prized, however, is their suitability for forcing.

Ixia L.

Iridaceae
16 to 24 in.
June

Ixias are distinguished for the bright colours of the small flowers which are not only decorative in the garden but also excellent for cutting. Their cultivation is limited though, because they are not really hardy, and the species native to southern Africa are rarely grown. However, a number of hybrids have been raised which can be cultivated more easily in sheltered locations. These generally flower from mid-June.

The round corm resembles that of gladiolus, the same being true of the leaves. The stem is slender and wiry and grows to a height of 16 to 24 in. depending on the variety. The star-shaped flowers, with six narrow or broad but always rounded petals are borne in spikes of six to ten flowers, opening only in the sun. The colour may be white, yellow, orange, pink to purple or scarlet. Only rarely is it uniform; as a rule the flower has a distinct darker purple, violet or black centre.

This plant should be grown in a warm, sunny position, preferably at the foot of a south-facing wall. A light sandy soil is best, and in winter the corms should be covered with leaves, bracken or peat. Propagation is by offsets from the corm, which are produced in sufficient number; the plant attains maturity in the second year. The corms should be planted in late autumn, best of all at the end of November, for otherwise they put out leaves which are damaged by frost in winter. They may remain in the ground for a number of years in warm, sheltered areas, otherwise they should be lifted annually. They are generally planted in small groups in flower beds.

Foxtail Lily
Eremurus M.B.

Liliaceae
1 to 9 ft.
May to June

Eremuri are tall plants native to the steppes of central and western Asia and entirely adapted to conditions there. The tongue-shaped leaves appear rapidly in spring to form a large rosette and the flowers appear in May to June. Broadly bell-shaped flowers ¾ to 2 in. across, with attractive, conspicuous, fairly long stamens, are borne in a large raceme on a stout stalk. The colour is white, yellow to orange or pink, depending on the species.

Eremurus robustus, native to Turkestan, is 8 to 9 ft. tall, with leaves about 2 ft. long. The flowers are borne in a large raceme which may be as much as 3 ft. long. The flower buds are salmon-pink, the open flowers somewhat paler to whitish tinged with pink.

The soil should be rich, well-drained and light, the site sunny, warm and sheltered. During the growing period in spring it requires abundant moisture; in summer and above all in winter, dry conditions. If the winter is a wet one it is easily killed by frost.

The species are propagated by means of seeds, which are produced in ample numbers. These should be sown as soon as ripe or in the autumn. Seedlings take about five years to develop. Varieties are propagated by division of the tuberous crowns in early autumn. The crowns have a large number of dormant buds and each separate piece should have at least one bud. Planting should be done straightaway and a protective cover should be given during the winter.

Eremuri, especially the tall species, may be planted only in gardens where there is plenty of space. They are most suitable in open groups in grass and in front of taller shrubs and conifers. They are also good as cut flowers in large vases in spacious rooms.

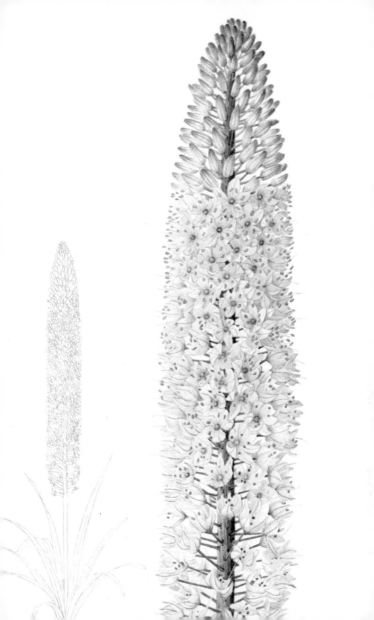

Eucomis comosa HORT. BEROL.

syn. *Eucomis punctata* (THUNB.) L'HERIT.

Liliaceae

2 to 3 ft.

July to August

Eucomis, native to southern Africa, is interesting more for its height than for the beauty of its flowers. It is one of those species which are planted only in small numbers or singly in the company of other, rather exotic plants and not in the wild garden.

The bulb is large and tunicated, the leaves basal, broadly lanceolate and spotted on the underside. The 2- to 3-ft. stems bear an upright conical raceme of small flowers with six equal perianth segments, generally creamy-white tinged with pink, surmounted by a small tuft of leaves like a pineapple, thus further accenting the exotic look.

The soil should be light, rich and well-drained and the site a warm, dry and sheltered location in full sun.

Propagation is by offsets from the bulb which take two to three years to develop or by means of seeds sown in pans in a cool greenhouse where they are slow to germinate. Seedlings bear flowers in the fourth year. The bulbs should be planted fairly deeply, some 5 to 6 in. Only in warmer areas may they be left in the ground for a number of years, in which case they should be provided with a good cover during the winter. They may also be lifted in the autumn, stored in a cool, dry place and put out again in early spring.

Galtonia candicans DECNE.

syn. *Hyacinthus candicans* BAK.

Liliaceae

2½ to 4 ft.

August

Galtonia is native to southern Africa, where it flowers in mid-December. In central Europe it flowers in August and is sometimes called summer hyacinth.

The bulb is large, round and white, the leaves, forming a ground rosette, are 1 to 2 ft. long, 2 to 2½ in. wide, fleshy, grey-green, later prostrate. The stem is 2½ to 4 ft. high with a loose raceme of drooping, bell-shaped flowers on long pedicels. The flowers are about 1½ in. long, ½ to ¾ in. wide and slightly scented. The colour is white, tinged with green.

Galtonia will grow in almost any location but does best in light, well-drained and nourishing soil. It requires a warm and sunny site and a light cover during the winter for it is not entirely frost-hardy.

Propagation is usually by means of seeds, which are produced in ample numbers. It is best to grow the seedlings in a green-house, where they generally flower the second year. Bulbs may be planted at the beginning of October or in early spring. Small bulbs should be planted about 5 in. deep, larger ones as much as 8 in. deep. If planted at a shallow depth they are easily destroyed by frost. Where possible they should be left in the ground for several years for they do not die back entirely and if undisturbed will produce nice strong plants.

Galtonia is suitable for group plantings in grass as well as in beds of perennials and is also good for cutting.

Turk's-cap Lily

Lilium martagon L.

This is one of the best-known species of lily for it is the most widespread, growing practically throughout the whole of Europe from Spain northward to southern Sweden and across Siberia. It thrives on lime soils, in semi-shaded locations, and grows even at elevations of 7,000 ft.

The bulb is yellow and made up of fleshy scales. The leaves are arranged in whorls on the stem which bears a thick raceme of pendulous, Turk's-cap flowers, about 2 in. across, on short pedicels. The colour of the flowers as well as the height of the plant show marked variation for there are many local forms throughout the vast range of its distribution.

The flowers may be soft pink with brownish-purple spots to a deep wine colour with few spots. (Very attractive but not as tall is the white form.) The flowers have a strong, rather unpleasant scent.

Lilium martagon requires well-drained, humus-rich soil with ample lime and semi-shade. Plant the bulbs about 4 in. deep, doing this after mid-September, as is the case with most lilies. The bulbs should be left for a number of years in the same spot, for it is only when they are mature that they produce a profusion of flowers.

Propagation is by division of the bulbs and by seeds. Plants raised from seed are slow to mature, seedlings often taking five years to flower.

This lily is not cultivated in large numbers, perhaps because of the fairly long time it takes to grow to flowering size, but it is very good in the wild or woodland garden in light shade.

Lilium regale WILS.

Although this lily was not discovered by E. H. Wilson in western China until 1903 it soon became one of the most popular and widespread in cultivation.

The bulb is reddish brown and made up of large fleshy scales. The leaves are narrow and arranged alternately on the 3- to 6-ft. stem. A sturdy plant may have from twelve to thirty funnel-shaped trumpet flowers about 5 in. across. These are white inside with a yellow throat, pink to carmine outside, mainly down the median stripe, and strongly fragrant.

It requires nourishing, well-drained soil and is tolerant of lime. It may be planted in the sun but shade should be provided for the ground surface. Full shade, however, is not suitable. This is a hardy lily.

Propagation is by means of seeds and division of the bulbs. It takes a comparatively short time to mature and the seedlings may flower in the second year. Mature bulbs should be planted 6 to 9 in. deep in September.

Because of the ease of cultivation this lily is a popular garden plant, though nowadays preference is given to many trumpet hybrids which also have a more delicate scent. It is suitable for planting in groups as well as in beds and is also used for cutting.

Lilium L.
cv. Enchantment

Liliaceac

2½ to 3 ft.

June

Lilies have always been flowers of great interest to gardeners. Many type species have special requirements and it is not always easy to grow and multiply them in the garden for years on end. In unsuitable locations they are prone to damage by pests and diseases. For this reason growers have focused their efforts on obtaining varieties that are just as or even more attractive than the species and are hardier and more adaptable to conditions in the normal garden.

One of the most popular of these garden varieties is 'Enchantment', selected by de Graaf in 1944 from the Mid Century Hybrids, a cross between *L. tigrinum* and *L.* × *hollandicum* belonging to Division Ia (early-flowering Asiatic hybrids with upright flowers). The stem is about 3 ft. high with an umbel of upturned, bowl-shaped flowers about 6 in. across. The colour is a bright nasturtium-red with brownish-red spots. This lily is readily propagated by means of the bulbils borne in the axils of the leaves. It does very well in the garden, being especially good in beds, and is also good for forcing.

Lilium L.
cv. Connecticut Glow

Liliaceae
2½ to 3½ ft.
July

The illustrated 'Connecticut Glow' is also one of the hybrids of Division Ia (Asiatic hybrids with upright flowers). Unlike 'Enchantment', now practically a classic of this group, 'Connecticut Glow' is one of the most recent members, a cross between 'Red Tiger' and 'Nubian', raised in 1967 by Stone and Payne.

It has a strong stem, 2½ to 3½ ft. high, with dark green leaves and eight to ten flowers which generally appear in mid-July.

The flowers are borne in an erect umbel on long pedicels. They are about 5 in. across, dark carmine outside and deeper carmine inside.

This is a variety that is yet to become widespread in cultivation. It seems to be fairly easy to grow and, like other Connecticut Hybrids, it should be planted in any good garden soil and in full sun. It, too, is suitable for group planting and for cutting.

Lilium L.
cv. Nutmegger

Liliaceae
4 to 4½ ft.
July

Lilies classed in Division I are mostly the rewarding hardy and fast-growing hybrids of the Asiatic species, particularly *L. amabile*, *L. davidii*, *L.* × *hollandicum* and *L. tigrinum*. They are divided into three divisions according to the position of the flowers. Division Ia has upright flowers ('Enchantment' — page 180), Division Ib horizontal flowers, and Division Ic, which includes 'Nutmegger', drooping flowers. 'Nutmegger' is an attractive, recent form, introduced in 1964 by Stone and Payne, with very good characteristics. It is quite hardy and does well even in full sun. The stem is 4 to 4½ ft. high with as many as thirty Turk's-cap flowers, 5 to 6 in. across, borne on fairly long pedicels in July. They are canary yellow with conspicuous dark brown spots over the entire inner surface.

'Nutmegger' is suitable for group plantings in beds and for cutting.

Lilium L.
cv. Golden Splendor

Liliaceae
3 to 6 ft.
July

'Golden Splendor', which belongs to Division VIa, is a strikingly coloured lily introduced by Ware in 1957 and one of the best of the de Graaf Golden Clarion Strain.

Attaining a height of up to 6 ft., the stem is thickly covered with leaves and bears eight to twenty five open, broadly trumpet-shaped flowers up to 6 in. across with slightly reflexed petals. They are a striking, warm yellow colour with conspicuous brownish-russet anthers. The bud is brownish purple and in the open flower the area round the median stripe is the same hue.

Golden Clarion Hybrids are among the lilies most highly prized by gardeners for they need no special care, requiring only soil with good drainage.

They may be planted, and are sure to do well, in any spot in the garden. They are also good for cutting.

Lilium L.
cv. Damson

'Damson' is a striking dark-coloured lily selected from the Aurelian Hybrids × *L. leucanthum* and raised by de Graaf in 1954. It belongs to Division VIa, namely Asiatic trumpet lily hybrids.

Reaching a height of 4 to 6 ft., the firm stem is thickly covered with ovate leaves, up to 4 in. long, and bears five to twenty flowers on 5-in. pedicels. These are broadly opened, long trumpets measuring 5 to 6 in. across and coloured a dark purplish-mauve with silvery tips that glow brightly in the sun.

This lily is likewise quite hardy and easy to grow and is one of the best clones in the group. It may be planted in a sunny position and, like all tall forms, it requires rich and well-drained soil.

It is suitable for group planting in beds and also for cutting.

Lilium L.
cv. Bright Star

Liliaceae
3 to 4 ft.
July

The lovely and delicate 'Bright Star' lily of Division VId is one
of the Aurelian Hybrids, based on crosses between *L. henryi* and
a trumpet lily, and raised by de Graaf.

It has a stout, brown-spotted stem 3 to 4 ft. high with alternate, lanceolate leaves and as many as fourteen or more flowers
borne horizontally on firm pedicels. The individual flowers,
5 to 6 in. in diameter, are flat and star-shaped, with broad,
slightly reflexed segments. They are almost white outside;
inside the apricot-orange star-shaped centre makes a lovely
contrast with the white margin.

This form is fairly hardy and easy to grow but like most other
lilies should be planted in rich, deep soil, best of all in semi-
shade. Bulbs should be planted 4 to 5 in. deep. It is readily
propagated by the bulbils which form up the stem.

It often happens that the stem is too weak to carry the weight
of a large number of flowers and should therefore be provided
with support by fastening it to a firm stake at several points.

Lilium L.
cv. Black Beauty

Liliaceae
5 to 8 ft.
August

'Black Beauty', belonging to Division VIId and raised in 1958 by Woodriff, is a cross between *L. speciosum punctatum* and *L. henryi*. It is a remarkable hybrid from the breeder's viewpoint for the parent species have totally opposite requirements as regards content of lime in the soil and it is believed that this variety may make it possible to overcome the difficulties of crossing Aurelian Hybrids with *L. speciosum* and *L. auratum* hybrids.

The stem is 5 to 8 ft. tall, and the Turk's-cap flowers, 4 to 5 in. across, are borne on long pedicels in large loose racemes containing as many as fifty flowers. They are a very deep red, almost blackish red towards the base, with a green star-shaped centre and delicate white border. The flowers are sterile and appear at the beginning of August. The underground stem produces a great number of bulblets.

This lily is very vigorous, generally robust, and will grow in almost any situation. It is planted in beds and may also be used for cutting.

Lilium L.
cv. Allegra

Division VII includes hybrids of eastern species, mainly *L. auratum* and *L. speciosum*. 'Allegra', raised in 1955 by S. L. Emsweller, belongs in section VIId, namely hybrids with recurved petals. It inherited the best characters of each of its parents — *L. speciosum album* and *L. auratum platyphyllum*. The long-pedicelled flowers are borne horizontally on a 5- to 6-ft. stem with abundant foliage. They are flat, up to 8 in. across, wavy at the edges and strongly recurved, white both inside and out, with a green star-shaped centre and prominent white papillae inside. They appear in August and have a pleasant scent.

This lily is considered one of the loveliest of the whole group.

The method of cultivation and uses are the same as for *L. speciosum* but it is more adaptable and may therefore be grown even in positions where *L. speciosum* does not do well.

194

Tiger Lily

Lilium tigrinum KER-GAWL.

The tiger lily is a well-known and often cultivated lily distinguished by the glossy black bulbils borne in the axils of the leaves. It is widespread in China, Japan and other parts of eastern Asia.

The bulb is white and composed of thick scales; the mature bulb measures about 3 in. across. The leaves are numerous, linear-lanceolate, dark green and glossy. Bulbils, which ripen and fall at about the time of flowering, appear in most leaf axils.

The stem may bear as many as twenty five Turk's-cap flowers about 4 in. across, which are coloured orange with a raspberry-pink tinge and conspicuous reddish-brown spots. They are not scented.

There are several varieties of *L. tigrinum* of varying shades and also a double form. *L. tigrinum* is frequently used for crossing with other species and played a part in the raising of the Mid Century Hybrids.

It is one of the least demanding of lilies but does not tolerate lime in the soil. It should be planted in full sun in rich soil and watered during the growing period. It is readily propagated by means of the bulbils but does not form seeds, for which reason it is generally used only as a father plant in hybridization. The bulbs should be planted about 8 in. deep in the second half of September.

The tiger lily is suitable for bedding and cutting.

Lilium henryi BAK.

Liliaceae
5 to 8 ft.
August to September

This is a fine Turk's-cap lily which is native to the mountains of Central China.

The bulb is large, sometimes as much as 8 in. across, dark reddish-brown, and composed of large fleshy scales. The leaves are dark green, lanceolate, about 6 in. long in the lower and middle parts of the stem, but markedly smaller near the top. The drooping, Turk's-cap flowers on long pedicels are borne in large racemes of fifteen to twenty flowers. The edges of the petals are frilled and there are prominent papillae, $\frac{1}{4}$ in. long, near the centre of the flower. The colour is orange-yellow to pale orange, sometimes pale green near the centre. It is not scented.

Lilium henryi will grow in almost any location with well-drained, humus-rich soil, but lime is a must; it will not thrive in acid soils. It is almost completely frost-resistant and may be planted in full sun though light shade is preferable.

It is easy to propagate, forming a great number of bulblets at the base and often spreading into large clumps. It is therefore necessary to divide the bulbs every three to four years. Bulbs should be planted 8 in. deep in September. Seeds are slow to germinate and do not grow into flower-bearing plants until the third year.

Lilium henryi is planted in small groups in beds and is also suitable for growing in the wild garden. The flowers are long-lived and are excellent for cutting. More commonly grown in recent years are its hybrids, for example the Aurelian Hybrids.

Lilium speciosum THUNB.

Liliaceae
2½ to 4½ ft.
August to September

This lily with its pleasant, sweet scent is doubtless one of the most beautiful of all lilies. It is native to Japan, being found on the island of Kyushu, where it generally grows at the edges of open woods.

The bulb is large, globose, russet-yellow, the scales broadly lanceolate and alternate. The Turk's-cap flowers on long pedicels are borne in large racemes sometimes numbering as many as twenty five. They are some 4 to 6 in. across, often waved at the edges, with prominent papillae near the centre. The colour is white with a crimson-pink tinge and crimson spots. There exist several differently coloured forms, such as *album* — almost white, *roseum* — pink, *rubrum* — one of the best known, coloured rich pink to crimson inside. *L. speciosum* itself is used for breeding purposes and more commonly cultivated nowadays are its hybrids, especially crosses with *L. auratum*.

L. speciosum requires a humus-rich, well-drained, non-calcareous soil combining a mixture of clay and sand to which some peat may be added. It should be planted in a sheltered position in semi-shade and provided with a light cover in winter. Damp in winter, not frost, is the prime cause of damage. It should also be sprayed at regular intervals to control the insects which spread virus diseases.

Propagation is by means of the scales and from seed, the latter taking four to five years to grow into flower-bearing plants. The bulbs should be planted about 9 in. deep; in a suitable sheltered position they may be left in the ground for a number of years.

Lilium speciosum is planted in groups in bedding schemes, is excellent for cutting and is sometimes also used for forcing. It has a lovely fragrance.

Gladiolus illyricus KOCH

Iridaceae
18 to 20 in.
June to July

This is a species gladiolus that grows wild in the Mediterranean regions, mostly in Dalmatia and Albania. It is not widely cultivated and is of interest only to the specialist gardener.

The stem is about 18 in. tall with narrow, sword-like leaves and a loose, one-sided spike of five to six fairly small flowers, about 1 in. across, coloured red to bright purple. The flowers generally appear in June.

Gladiolus illyricus is fairly hardy but it is best to plant it in a sheltered, warm and sunny situation. Like most other species gladioli it may be left in the ground for the winter whereas garden varieties must always be lifted in the autumn. Even though type species are hardier they generally require a protective cover for the winter.

Propagation is by cormlets or by means of seed.

Gladiolus illyricus is suitable for planting in small groups in the wild garden together with other bulbous and tuberous plants.

Gladiolus L.

cv. Jan Voerman

Iridaceae

2 to 2½ ft.

July to September

Even with the great increase of large-flowered varieties, gladioli of the Primulinus group have remained popular favourites. The type species *G. primulinus* is native to tropical Africa, has a 2½-ft. stem, which is generally crooked, and small, yellow, characteristically shaped flowers that are not especially attractive. The upper petal is curved down and inward and protects the reproductive organs from drying out. The down-curved petal as well as the yellow colouring is easily passed on to the offspring in cross-breeding. It was used for breeding purposes as early as the eighteenth century for its yellow colour.

The variety 'Jan Voerman' of unknown parentage also has this characteristically shaped flower. However, the stem is up to 2½ ft. tall and the flowers, 3 in. across, are arranged in a looser spike about 16 in. long with seventeen buds and four florets open at the same time. The colour is vermilion, with a large, deep red, yellow-rimmed blotch on the lower petals. It is easily propagated and flowers early.

This variety is planted in beds and is used primarily for cutting.

Gladiolus L.
cv. Pink Sensation

Iridaceae
2½ to 3½ ft.
July to September

Garden varieties of gladiolus are of very mixed origin, being derived from both European and African species. Countless new varieties are raised every year, most of them soon falling into oblivion. Over the years only those that are healthy, readily propagated and can be relied on to produce flowers retain their foothold; particular stress is laid on the aesthetic factor only in the case of newly introduced forms. Though the number raised equals some 100,000 only about 20,000 forms are found in cultivation nowadays. The assortment grown in Europe differs markedly from that cultivated in America and similarly, the selection offered by horticultural establishments, apart from the standard favourites, shows marked variation.

The most numerous group are the large-flowered gladioli with either smooth or waved edges. In catalogues they are often divided into three sections according to the period of flowering — namely, early, mid-season and late-flowering gladioli. The range of colours is very wide and forms are grown either in pure colours or with variously coloured blotches inside the flowers.

'Pink Sensation' is a late, large-flowered form with big florets, 4 to 4½ in. across, borne in a fairly dense spike. They are soft pink with a large, creamy-white blotch marked with purple.

Gladiolus L.
cv. Blue Diamond

Iridaceae
3 to 4 ft.
July to September

Highly prized by gardening enthusiasts are the blue forms of gladiolus, many of which, however, are difficult to propagate. 'Blue Diamond' (raised by Barret) of the large-flowered group is one of the blue forms that multiply fairly readily. It flowers quite early, measures 3 to 4 ft. in height, and has a dense, 20-in. spike. A mature corm bears eighteen buds and generally at least five open florets at a time. The flowers are $4\frac{1}{2}$ in. across and the edges are slightly waved. The ground colour is blue with a faint silvery sheen and a large, creamy-yellow blotch on the lower petals with narrow, spotted, violet-blue markings in the centre.

This form, like other garden varieties, is planted in groups at the back of beds of perennials but is more often used for cutting. In beds it is a good idea to plant the very tall varieties at a greater depth than normal (that is about 5 in. deep), as at least partial protection against their being uprooted.

Gladiolus L.
cv. Mexico

Iridaceae
4 ft.
July to September

The beautiful, large-flowered Mexico gladiolus was raised in 1957 by Roberts. It is a robust form up to 4 ft. in height with a firm, tall straight spike bearing eighteen buds and often as many as eight open florets at a time. The flowers are large, often more than 5 in. across, broadly expanded, bright pinkish-red with a narrow, pale yellow blotch inside. They appear fairly late.

'Mexico', like other varieties with very large flowers, is best suited for cutting, being placed in large vases and often used for ceremonial occasions. The usual arrangement is in bouquets of a single colour, especially varieties with markedly different blotches or very wavy edges.

One drawback to these gladioli when growing them in the garden is that, although they have firm stems, they are easily uprooted. For this reason it is a good idea to tie each stem loosely to a bamboo cane for support.

Gladiolus L.
cv. D'Artagnan

Iridaceae
$2\frac{1}{2}$ to 4 ft.
July to September

Very popular in the garden are the large-flowered varieties with a conspicuous blotch. One such is 'D'Artagnan' (raised by Konijnenburg and Mark), a fairly early form. It is quite a robust plant, up to 4 ft. tall, with a compact, $1\frac{3}{4}$-ft. spike bearing nineteen buds and five open florets at a time. The firm flowers measure $4\frac{1}{2}$ in. across and are broadly expanded. They are creamy-white to pale yellow or pinkish with a large red blotch rimmed with yellow on the lower petals. In the case of such brightly coloured forms best effects are achieved if they are used alone.

This is a healthy variety which is easily propagated. All garden varieties are propagated by means of cormlets or better still offsets as described in the section on propagation. They should always be lifted in the autumn and stored for the winter in a dry room with temperature of 43 to 50°F. (6 to 10°C.). April is the time for putting out the corms; offsets should be planted as soon as possible, best of all in March, for they are often slow to start into growth.

Tiger Flower

Tigridia pavonia KER-GAWL.

Iridaceae
1 to 2 ft.
July to September

Tigridia is a striking exotic flower which derives its name from its bright colouring and tiger-like spots. *T. pavonia*, and its hybrids, is the only one of the about twelve described species to be widely grown. It is native to Mexico, Guatemala and Peru, where it grows in damp situations at elevations up to 6,000 ft. It was introduced into Europe as early as the sixteenth century.

The corm is firm, ovoid, about 4 in. in circumference, and covered with a coarse tunic. The leaves are pale green, fairly narrow and plicate. The height is 2 ft. at the most and the erect, branched stem bears as many as six flowers which open successively one after the other. Each flower lasts only a single day, opening in the morning and fading in the evening. They are fairly big, some 4 to 6 in. across, and have three large and three smaller petals very variable in colour, ranging from scarlet, orange to yellow as well as crimson, purple, pink and white, spotted yellow or purple on a pale ground inside.

Tigridia requires a loose, well-drained, humus-rich soil, a sheltered site in full sun and plenty of moisture. It is not hardy and should generally be lifted for the winter except in very mild places. Cultivation is the same as for gladioli. It should be planted in April or early May, covering the corms with 3 in. of soil. The corms can be started into growth in a frame, the plants being put out when they are 2 to 3 in. high.

Propagation is by means of cormlets or seeds, which are produced in great numbers. The seed should be sown in a frame in early spring and with good care may grow to flowering size the very first year.

Tigridia pavonia is usually planted in sheltered beds in small groups.

Montbretia

Crocosmia × *crocosmiiflora* N. E. BROWN
syn. *Montbretia crocosmiiflora* LEMOINE

Iridaceae
2 to 3 ft.
August to
September

Montbretias are native to South Africa and are not completely hardy in cold areas. *C.* × *crocosmiiflora*, a cross between *C. aurea* and *C. pottsii*, is hardier than the type species.

The corms, resembling those of the crocus, are small with a firm tunic which sometimes becomes ragged at the edges. The leaves are sword-like and arranged on the stem like those of gladiolus. The stem with inflorescence is sometimes as much as 3 ft. high. The flowers are borne in a loose panicle 6 to 8 in. long. They are funnel- to bell-shaped. The colour is generally orange-red but there are also forms coloured scarlet to crimson and pale orange to yellow.

The soil should be light, well drained and rich and the site a sheltered and sunny location. Only in such a spot can it remain outdoors for the winter, though even so it is a good idea to provide it with a protective cover. In less favourable conditions the corms should be lifted in the autumn and given the protection of a cold frame until the following April when they should be split up and replanted. If they are not lifted for the winter they should be transplanted every three years. Propagation is generally by cormlets, which should be planted out in April about 2 to 3 in. deep and which take two years to develop. It is also possible to raise plants from the seed, but in this case they will not come true to type.

Montbretias flower successively over a long period and even if the flowers are not very long-lived their glowing colours make them popular plants for bedding and also for cutting.

Cyclamen europaeum L.

Primulaceae
3 to 4 in.
July to September

Cyclamen are among the most popular flowers for the rock garden. Most species of this genus are native to Europe, especially the wooded mountain regions round the Mediterranean. Only *C. europaeum* is found also north of the Alps, where it flowers in late summer. The tuber is round and corky on the outside. Growing from the tuber is a ground rosette of persistent, kidney-shaped leaves with silvery white markings on the upper surface and dark red below. The flowers, borne on 2- to 3-in. stems, are single, with five recurved petals forming a small mouth in the centre. The petals are coloured purplish-pink, the mouth dark red. Cyclamen flower in August to September and have a very pleasant fragrance.

The soil should be a mixture of clay and sand, rich in humus and with good drainage. The location should be warm but provided with semi-shade or shade. Although this cyclamen is native to central Europe, in cold gardens it is wise to provide it with a light cover during the winter.

Propagation is from seed which should be sown in pans in July to August. It takes two years for them to develop. Tubers should be planted in August $\frac{3}{4}$ to 1 in. deep, in other words at a rather shallow depth. They should not be moved often for they require at least two years to become established. When transplanting the tubers they should be returned to the ground as soon as possible in order to prevent them from drying out. They are planted primarily in sheltered and shaded sites in the rock garden and in groups under trees and shrubs.

Cyclamen neapolitanum TEN.
syn. *Cyclamen hederaefolium* AIT.

Primulaceae

4 to 5 in.

August to September

This cyclamen is considered one of the best. It is native to southern Italy and Greece and grows wild also in regions bordering the Mediterranean. It flowers in late summer (August to September), the same as *C. europaeum*, which it greatly resembles both in size and shape of the flower.

The tubers are large and flat, saucer-shaped and corky on the outside. The roots are produced only from the upper surface, where also the short branches from which the flowers grow are produced. The leaves are very ornamental and very variable in shape and patterning. They are obcordate, with silvery markings that are generally very conspicuous. The flower is about the same size as that of *C. europaeum*, differing only in the shape of the mouth which is not round but pentagonal, and a deeper shade of red. The colour is pink or purplish pink and there is also a white form. Unlike *C. europaeum*, *C. neapolitanum* is not scented.

Requirements are the same as for *C. europaeum*. It should be planted in semi-shade, though it also tolerates sun, and benefits from light protection in winter.

Propagation is by means of seeds. When planting tubers it is necessary to remember that in this species roots are produced from the upper surface. For this reason the tubers should be planted about 4 in. deep and the right way up. This species is intolerant of frequent transplanting, and often fails to flower the first year after planting. Strong, old tubers may produce more than thirty flowers.

Uses are the same as for *C. europaeum*.

Colchicum L.

Liliaceae
6 to 10 in.
August to October

Colchicums are widespread primarily in southern Europe. At one time the greatest number grew in the region of Colchis in Asia Minor, hence their name. Some species are also found in western and central Asia and North Africa. The only species that is widespread throughout the whole of Europe is *C. autumnale*, which grows in damp meadows. All parts of the plant contain the very toxic alkaloid colchicin used in the pharmaceutical industry and in modern methods of plant breeding.

The tuber is unsymmetrically shaped and covered with a brown coat. The leaves, which do not appear until spring, are generally large, elongate and variable in width, depending on the species. The flowers have six perianth segments that are joined to form a long tube extending to the ovary close to the tuber. The various species flower from August to October. The flowers are coloured varying shades of violet-pink and in some species have mosaic or chequered markings. There are also white and double forms.

Colchicums require deep and rich soil, some also need plenty of moisture. They do best in the sun but will tolerate slight shade.

They are readily propagated by means of offsets of the tuber which reach flower-bearing size in the second year. Large tubers should be planted in July to August 4 to 8 in. deep. Species colchicums can also be propagated from seed.

They are best planted in grass, which, however, should not be cut too soon, so that the foliage can die down.

Colchicum hybridum HORT.

Liliaceae
6 to 10 in.
August to October

Autumn-flowering colchicums definitely deserve a place in the garden and thus they, too, could not but become the object of experiments by breeders who are always trying to raise new, large-flowered and free-flowering forms that are readily propagated. The greatest number of hybrids have been raised from crosses between *C. sibthorpii* and *C. speciosum*, and the ones most widely grown are 'Lilac Wonder', 'The Giant', 'Violet Queen' and 'Water Lily'.

'Violet Queen', shown in the illustration, is purplish pink with a narrow white stripe in the throat. It is about 6 in. tall and flowers in September.

Garden varieties generally require a richer soil. Like the type species they, too, are intolerant of frequent transplanting. On the contrary, not till after several years in one site do they flower really profusely. However, they do require the addition of fertilizer now and then. If they are being transferred to a different site the period of storage should be as short as possible.

Varieties are propagated only by offsets from the tuber. Mature tubers are generally large, as much as 10 in. in circumference, and therefore should be planted 6 to 8 in. deep, either in grass or near the rock garden but always in a spot where their big leaves will not be in the way in spring.

Crocus byzantinus KER-GAWL.

Iridaceae

syn. *Crocus iridiflorus* HEUFF.

4 to 6 in.

September to October

This lovely autumn crocus is comparatively rare in cultivation for efforts to grow it do not always meet with success. However, in locations where it does well it may even spread freely by self-sown seedlings.

It grows wild in eastern Europe, mainly Hungary, Bulgaria and Romania.

The corms are fairly small, globose, with fibrous tunic. The leaves are long, comparatively broad and without the prominent silvery streak on the surface. The flowers are unusual in that the outer segments are considerably larger than the inner ones. They may be nearly 2 in. long whereas the inner segments are never longer than 1 in. They are broadly oval and all terminate in a point. The outer segments are coloured pale violet blue, the inner ones silvery blue at the tip, otherwise almost white. The stigmata are light purple and faintly segmented.

Crocus byzantinus is a hardy crocus but requires a suitable permanent site where it can become established. It should be supplied with light shade, for in its native habitat it often grows in thin, open woodlands, and the soil should be slightly acid and moister than for other species of crocus.

Propagation is by offsets of the corm and from seed. The cormlets should be planted in August, 2 to 3 in. deep.

Crocus byzantinus is excellent planted in grass, near trees and shrubs as well as in the rock garden.

Crocus speciosus M. B.

Iridaceae
5 to 6 in.
September to October

The growing popularity of autumn-flowering crocuses may perhaps be attributed to their being the heralds of a new spring. Many of them flower in autumn but do not put out leaves until spring, which is also when the seed ripens.

Crocus speciosus is the commonest and most widespread species. It grows in the Balkans, Asia Minor and Afghanistan.

The corms are large, globose, with an annulate tunic. The leaves generally do not appear until spring. The flowers, about 2½ in. across, have six fairly narrow, elongate, bluntly-tipped perianth segments joined to form a long tube. The colour is usually light blue with darker prominent veins, yellow throat, orange stigmata and yellow anthers. Seedlings have very variable colouring. A number of forms of diverse shades have been selected and named and there is also a white form.

Crocus speciosus is an undemanding species and will grow well in light, well-drained soil in the sun. It may be planted in grass though it loses its vigour after a number of years and new corms must be added. It is also good for the rock garden.

Propagation is by offsets from the corm, especially in the case of pure-coloured forms. The type species may be propagated from seed which grows to flower-bearing size in three to four years. The cormlets should be planted 2½ to 3 in. deep in October.

Nerine bowdenii W. WATS.

Amaryllidaceae
16 to 24 in.
October to November

Nerine bowdenii, native to South Africa, is a very decorative bulb flowering in late autumn. It is large and brightly coloured and in favourable conditions may be planted out in the open, though it is more commonly grown in a cool greenhouse.

The bulbs are round, fairly large, white, and composed of thin layers. The leaves are narrow, strap-shaped, and coloured pale green. The first leaves appear together with the flowers but last until the following summer. The stem may be up to 2 ft. tall and is terminated by an umbel generally consisting of eight flowers. The petals are about 3 in. long, fairly narrow, with reflexed margins. The colour is pink with a darker line down the inside of each segment. Also cultivated are several varieties of different shades and different shape of flower.

Of all the nerines, only *N. bowdenii* is planted out in the open. However, even this species requires a warm, sheltered and sunny location, best of all under a south-facing wall. The soil should be light, rich and well drained.

The bulbs should be planted about 6 in. deep in autumn or winter, and a protective cover of dry leaves or peat is a must during the winter months. They should be transferred only when they become too congested and flower poorly. *N. bowdenii* is readily propagated by offsets from the bulb but may also be increased from seed. If grown in pots the bulbs should be planted at a shallow depth with the neck of the bulb above the soil. After the leaves have died down the bulbs require a period of complete rest and watering should not be resumed until the flower buds appear.

Nerine bowdenii is a beautiful bulb for planting in warm beds close to the house. The longevity of the flowers when used for cutting makes it a very valuable plant.

Bibliography

Anderson E. B. Hardy Bulbs. Vol. 1. Middlesex 1964

Baranova M. V. Hyacint. Moscow 1964

Beck C. Fritillaries. London 1953

Bochanceva Z. P. Tiulpany — morfologiia, citologiia i biologiia. Tashkent 1962

Bowles E. A. A Handbook of Crocus and Colchicum for Gardeners. London 1952

Classified List and International Register of Daffodil Names. London 1969

Classified List and International Register of Hyacinths and Other Bulbous and Tuberous-Rooted Plants. Haarlem 1963

Classified List and International Register of Tulip Names. Hillegom 1971

Coleman C. F. Hardy Bulbs. Vol. 2. Middlesex 1964

Feldmaier C. Die neuen Lilien. Stuttgart 1967

Gray A. Miniature Daffodils. London 1961

Grunert C. Das große Bluemenzwiebelbuch. Berlin 1968

Hall A. D. The Genus Tulipa. London 1940

Hay R., Synge P. M. The Dictionary of Garden Plants. London 1972

Holitscher O. Průhonický sortiment tulipánů. Acta Průh. 18. 1968 — Průhonický sortiment tulipánů. II. Acta Průh. 26. 1972

Jefferson—Brown M. J. Daffodils and Narcissi. London 1969

Rockwell F. F., Grayson E. C., de Graaf J. The Complete Book of Lilies. New York 1961

Rodionienko, G. I. Rod Iris L. Moscow-Leningrad 1961

Smrž O. Dějiny růží a květin. Chrudim 1923—24

Synge P. M. Collins Guide to Bulbs. London 1961

The International Lily Register. London 1969

Zalivskii I. L.   Liliyi. Leningrad 1959

Zander R.   Handwörterbuch der Pflanzennamen. Stuttgart 1964

Index